Parents often have little time to prepare for fa
lead their families with God's Word. This gu
a concise analysis of the day's reading fro
minutes, helpful guidelines for age-appropria
or hymn to sing, and a starting point for family prayer. What a help and what a
blessing!

Dr Joel R. Beeke
President,
Puritan Reformed Theological Seminary,
Grand Rapids, Michigan

Since publishing The Family Worship Book (Christian Focus Publications, 1998),
a common concern expressed by heads of households is that they struggle to
get started. They are unsure of what exactly to do, when, and for how long. Help
has arrived! Geoff Gleason's new work takes those leading family worship step-
by-step, from Scripture reading, to family devotion, to singing God's praises, to
concluding prayer. The older Protestant authors frequently urge the practice of
what they called "family religion," seeing it as a vital plank in God's program for
the revival of vital Christianity. May we see a renewal in our day of this much
neglected spiritual discipline, as Gleason guides the "little churches" that meet
in homes through the Gospel of Luke.

Terry L. Johnson,
Senior Minister,
Independent Presbyterian Church,
Savannah, Georgia

Family worship serves as one of the greatest encouragements to faith and
godliness in the Christian family. Few of us need to be convinced of this truth,
but the realities of practicing family worship often make these benefits seem
distant or even inaccessible. We aren't sure what to say about a passage, how
to apply the text in an age-appropriate way, or even what to pray. That is why I
am thankful for this guide by Geoff Gleason. As a seasoned pastor and father,
he gently and helpfully takes the reader by the hand and simplifies the practice
of family worship. Use this guide and bless your family with the eternal benefits
that flow from centering your home upon the Word and prayer.

Jason Helopoulos,
Associate Pastor,
University Reformed Church,
East Lansing, Michigan

—| LUKE |—

GEOFF GLEASON

CHRISTIAN
FOCUS

paperback ISBN 978-1-5271-0040-4
epub ISBN 978-1-5271-0075-6
mobi ISBN 978-1-5271-0076-3

10 9 8 7 6 5 4 3 2 1

Published in 2017
by
Christian Focus Publications Ltd,
Geanies House, Fearn, Ross-shire,
IV20 1TW, Great Britain.

www.christianfocus.com

Cover design by
Paul Lewis

Printed and bound by
Bell and Bain, Glasgow

MIX
Paper from
responsible sources
FSC® C007785

Contents

This volume, written for the glory of God, is written with profound gratitude to the following people:

My dear wife Lisa who encourages me in my work as a father like no one else; my wonderful eleven children who all endure my growing pains in practicing family worship; my father and mother, Ron and Sally Gleason, who modeled this discipline for me; Janet Hanger and John van Eyk who willingly proof-read this work while it was in production mode, and finally Dave and Beccy Kennedy whom the Lord used to impact my life in a way still being felt by me every day though we have lived far apart for fifteen years. Thank you all for what you mean to me.

Series Introduction

GOD, in His Word, tells His people they have the glorious privilege of presenting their bodies as living sacrifices, holy and acceptable to Him, as a spiritual act of worship. This worship is only possible for those in whom God's Spirit dwells. But when He enters in, we can be certain that heartfelt worship will flow from each regenerated heart. For those who are made new in Christ, worship is a joyful privilege. As God works in the hearts of His people, He does more than simply direct them to a vague duty. God in His wisdom shows us what we are to believe about Him and how we should live as His people. Worship, in all of life, is that combination of knowledge and action performed for the glory and honor of God.

The joy of worship may belong to the believer, but in his life there is also an ever-present tension. Through years of pastoral experience and the discussions I have had with many serious and godly fathers, and by looking at my own life, I know that the world, the flesh, and the devil all tempt us to neglect the joyful task of worship. Jesus Himself warns us of this forgetfulness in the Olivet Discourse when He gives the parable of the talents. In that parable, two servants remember they are serving their master on borrowed time as his stewards. One servant prefers to serve himself. This series seeks to help develop your practice of worship by providing the structure that makes daily Bible study easier, while at the same time doing some of the legwork of explanation and application. In doing so, the hope is that you will be encouraged to take up your Bible daily for the benefit of your own soul, and for the benefit of your family.

Regular Bible study with your family, or what is commonly called family worship, is the best thing you can do to prepare your children for adulthood. There is no greater gift God gives to anyone than the grace of salvation through faith. Parents have the great joy and delight of serving the Lord in setting the gospel before their children, each day. As the glory of the gospel takes hold of your heart, you have the privilege of passing it on to your family. Deuteronomy 6:6-7 teaches, 'And these words that I command you today shall be on your heart. You shall teach them diligently to your children, and shall talk of them when you sit in your house, and when you walk by the way, and when you lie down, and when you rise.' God teaches us here that there is both a teaching and modeling aspect to a parent. Not only are parents to lead their families in worship through God's Word, but as parents we have the privilege of setting before our children an example to be followed. I can tell you from experience, there is great joy in sitting together with your family, reading and studying God's Word, thinking through what that means for daily living, praying together, and singing His praises.

Of course, the weakness of our flesh makes consistency in family worship challenging. This series hopes to help make family worship an easier practice to maintain. Through the regular practice of gathering your family before Almighty God, you will have the chance to be instrumental in shaping your child's knowledge and understanding about the Lord. As you work through the different books in this series, you will be sure to cover the whole breadth of teaching of the Bible. To help you get there, keep the following practical suggestions in mind:

- As much as possible, have family worship the same time every day;
- Choose a time where your whole family is naturally together, for example mealtime;
- Be sensitive to your children's attention span and understanding of biblical teaching. Begin small, with a goal toward growth;
- In prayer ask God to bless you as you study His Word together.

So begin, or continue the adventure of family worship! Read God's Word, understand God's Word, but then also lead your family in living God's Word. It is your spiritual act of worship to give glory to God.

GEOFF GLEASON
Series Editor

How to use this manual

THIS manual is put together to assist you in leading your family in the worship of the great God of Scripture. Each lesson has the same structure, and knowing it will help you use this series to its maximum potential.

Today's Reading. This is the most important part of each lesson in this book. Faithfully reading Scripture to your family will be of more help to them than anything in these volumes. Read in such a way that your children recognize how significant God's word is to you. Then the rest of the lesson is meant to supplement and facilitate discussion with your children and you seek to train them up in the fear of the Lord.

Introduction. Each lesson begins with a brief summary of the main point of the section of Scripture being considered. Knowing this main point will help you direct the conversation during family worship.

Bible Teaching. This section breaks the passage down into different parts and contains a brief explanation of each. It will briefly explain any difficult sections that may arise and also show how the main idea of the passage is developed in the different parts.

Family Discussion. Sometimes it is difficult to begin a conversation. This section is meant to give some starting points for discussions with your children, with different questions for children with different maturities. Naturally, if your children have other questions, pursue and answer those first. Feel free to mix and borrow from the different sections if you think that may be helpful.

Family Singing. Part of family worship should be singing together, although not everyone is gifted in this area. This series seeks to help build your family repertoire of hymns and psalms. Each volume will rotate its own small selection of hymns and songs. The hymns have been taken from the *Trinity Hymnal* published by Great Commission Publications. The psalms have been selected from *The Book of Psalms for Worship* produced by Crown & Covenant Publications. Naturally, other songs may be used to replace or supplement these selections.

Family Prayer. One of the best ways to teach your children to pray is to pray with them. As they see and hear you pray, you model what prayer looks like. Ask them to pray as part of family worship so they can grow in this discipline. To help with prayer, this section gives some suggestions related to the lesson for the day.

To lead your family well in worship requires preparation. This book is designed to help with this study. But remember: the value in family worship is not found in the profundity of your lesson, but rather in your commitment to setting God's word before your family every day. May God bless you as you honor him in the eyes of your family.

CHAPTER 1

A Great Promise and Great Doubt

TODAY'S READING: LUKE 1:1-25.

Introduction

As we open the book and consider its purpose we first learn about the trust-worthiness of the Word of God. Luke, seeking to reassure his Gentile friend Theophilus, begins with the reliability of God's message.

Bible Teaching

This section of Scripture can be divided up in the following way:

◀ 1:1-4. Luke is written as a Gospel, which means good news. There are four such Gospels in the Bible. These books are not meant to be a biography or history of Jesus. Rather, the Gospel writer selects events or teachings from Jesus' life to reveal and confirm Him as the prophesied Messiah. Luke's purpose comes out clearly in verse 4, as it records his stated purpose: to reinforce things previously taught to Theophilus regarding the Lord Jesus Christ. The rest of the book shows that Jesus is the predicted Messiah and that He certainly has accomplished what He was sent to do.

◀ 1:5-25. Luke is unique among the Bible's four Gospels in the details he gives about John the Baptist, including his birth. Luke's first narrative is not about the Messiah, but about His forerunner. Luke begins with a sense of expectation in verses 5-11. Zechariah and Elizabeth are righteous and blameless, but they had not been blessed with children. Though God withheld children, He grants Zechariah the privilege of performing the task of burning incense in the temple. This task was only given to each priest once in his lifetime and brought him as close as he would ever get to the Most Holy Place.

In Zechariah's interaction with the angel in verses 12-23, note 400 years have passed since God gave special revelation to the people of Israel. But now an angel appears to Zechariah and immediately calms his fears with gracious words. The announcement is joyful for Zechariah on a personal level (v. 14) and the people of Israel more generally (v. 17). Yet Zechariah is punished because he disbelieved an angel delivering a message to him from God. We may disbelieve men, but disbelieving God's messengers is like disbelieving God Himself. As a result of his doubt, Zechariah is unable to speak and is left incapable of fulfilling his privileged task.

Just as the punishment is applied immediately, so is the promise in verses 24-25. Elizabeth conceives and understands the fruit of her womb is a blessing from the Lord.

Family Discussion

Today consider the trustworthiness of the Word of God. Where Zechariah doubted, depend on God to give the grace to trust.

Little Children: Talk about what it means to believe in something. Show their trust for you when they jump to you from the stairs. Show how they can trust God's Word that way and that they should never doubt it.

Middle Children: Later in Luke 9:21-22, Jesus predicts His death and resurrection, yet the disciples do not believe Him (cf. Matt. 28:17). Show how man's response to God's promises is often faithless, rather than of faith. Discuss the importance of trusting God's Word.

Older Children: Look at Hebrews 11:1 and discuss the life of faith of the Christian. Discuss how Christianity is not a religion of blind faith but rather one of trust in the revealed Word of God. Look at a passage like Matthew 6:33 and ask whether they truly believe this promise of God or if their attitude is more like Zechariah's.

Family Singing

How Firm a Foundation (Trinity Hymnal #94); O Lord, Our Lord (Psalter #8A)

Family Prayer

Pray for an increase in faith for your family and a confidence in God's Word. Ask for the churches of Christ to be strengthened in the proclamation of this certain Word.

CHAPTER 2

The Promised King

TODAY'S READING: LUKE 1:26-56.

Introduction

One of the great mysteries of God and His work is the Incarnation. We are unable to fully grasp the mystery of the second person of the Trinity taking on human flesh and becoming like us in every way except for sin. Even the greatest theologians have wrestled with this topic and struggled to explain it fully. However, though we cannot explain the Incarnation, today we join the rest of the saints in marveling at it.

Bible Teaching

We can divide our passage between the three main narratives it records. Each involves Mary and the promised arrival of Jesus.

◀ 1:26-38. In this section the angel announces Jesus' birth to Mary. Although the Old Testament Davidic line of kings had long lain dormant, the Scripture assures us of the abiding significance of his house. Through God's progressive revelation He continually clarifies the identity of the family of the Redeemer first promised in Genesis 3:15. Both in His promise to David in 2 Samuel 7:12-14 and Gabriel's message to Mary God promises three things: first, a son on the throne, second, a rule established by God, and third, an everlasting reign. This Promised One will be borne in an unimaginable way; He will take on human flesh through the working of the Holy Spirit. Though our ability to fully comprehend this truth is limited, we trust God's Word lest we be reproved like Job when he questions God's ways (cf. Job 38:2).

◀ 1:39-45. In Mary's visit to Elizabeth, the latter is filled with the Holy Spirit, unusual for the time preceding Pentecost. However, although unusual, it is not unprecedented. In the Old Testament, the Holy Spirit is referenced 72 times (eg. Gen. 1:2; Judges 3:10; 1 Sam. 10:6). Under His inspiration, Elizabeth sings a song of praise to the Lord. This song is the first of five songs Luke records in response to the Incarnation. The others are Mary's song (1:46-56), Zechariah's prophecy (1:67-79), the angels' song (2:14), and Simeon's song (2:29-32). Elizabeth's song is not about Mary. She is simply the vessel. Mary's significance has to do with the One she carries.

◀ 1:46-56. In Mary's song, the 2nd response to the Incarnation, she turns away from man's achievements to stand in awe of the work of the Lord. While praising God for the splendor of His work in redemption, the song mainly contrasts the humble with the proud. Humility does not lead to redemption, but we are humbled as God redeems us.

Family Discussion
Help your family see how awesome God's work is in bringing Jesus into the world.

Little Children: Ask your children what they like about Christmas. Depending on the answer, either reinforce the amazing truth of the Incarnation, or show them how much greater the Incarnation is than grandparent visits and presents.

Middle Children: Talk about what it means to walk humbly before the Lord and Mary's humble response to being chosen by God to carry Christ in her womb. Talk about ways you can practice humility.

Older Children: In verse 50 Mary says God's mercy 'is for those who fear him.' Discuss the difference between the slavish fear of the unbeliever who fears God's judgment and the childlike fear of the believer who stands in awe before the Lord because of His undeserved work of salvation.

Family Singing
Great King of Nations, Hear Our Prayer (Trinity Hymnal #713); O Lord, Our Lord (Psalter #8A)

Family Prayer
Thank the Lord for His condescension in the redemption of man. Ask God to help you always remember the Incarnation with awe.

CHAPTER 3

John the Baptist Is Born

TODAY'S READING: LUKE 1:57-80.

Introduction

Luke's Gospel account is like building a block tower. Each new block contributes to the whole. John's birth reminds us of Gabriel's visit with Zechariah at the temple. Though Zechariah's initial response was doubt, Luke gives Theophilus a new block, demonstrating proper fear for the Lord in Zechariah's final response. Part of this fear is expressed in song. If Elizabeth's song on the Incarnation is one of joy and Mary's of awe, Zechariah's focuses on God's faithfulness.

Bible Teaching

As you work your way through the significance of the Incarnation, the birth of John the Baptist is an important event. Look at the implications of his birth in these two sections today.

◀ 1:57-66. John's arrival hints at what will separate him from the people of his day. The concern of the neighbors is with tradition. They expect Zechariah and Elizabeth to give their son a traditional family name. Certainly they knew of the angel's announcement of his birth. Yet when Elizabeth names the child according to the angel's instruction, her family and friends appeal to Zechariah. However, the aged priest is not willing to question God's instructions anymore and confirms Elizabeth's choice. In response to Zechariah's obedience, his tongue is loosed again, and he uses it to sing his song of praise for God's faithfulness.

◀ 1:67-79. Zechariah's song, called the Benedictus (from the Latin word for 'blessed' which opens his song), speaks of God's faithfulness, first to His people and then, specifically, to John. The first half of the song (vv. 68-75) deals with the Lord's blessing on His people. Zechariah makes three observations about God's blessing: first, God's faithfulness saves us from our enemies (v. 71); second, God's faithfulness rests on His ancient covenant promises to Abraham and the other patriarchs (vv. 72-73); and third, God's faithfulness enables us to serve Him in 'holiness and righteousness' (vv. 74-75). The second half of the song (vv. 76-79) deals with God's faithfulness to John.

He is the last prophet that anticipates the Messiah and, as such, is the last Old Testament prophet. His task will be to call Israel back to a proper understanding of salvation. In doing so he will enlighten the paths of the people again.

Family Discussion

John's birth and Zechariah's song show the faithfulness of God from which the following implications for daily living can be drawn.

Little Children: Talk about Zechariah and Elizabeth's obedient response in naming their son John. Talk about how they obey God because they love His promises to them. Talk about the importance of thankful obedience to God.

Middle Children: Review the three songs of response to the Incarnation recorded by Luke so far (cf. Elizabeth's song in 1:42-45, Mary's song in 1:46-55, and today's Benedictus). Talk about how God's faithfulness should make our obedience to Him joyful. Discuss how we can take God's faithfulness for granted in our response to His promises.

Older Children: Talk about the freedom purchased for us by Christ in His faithful work. Show how the Christian is not set free to self-indulge (cf. Gal. 5:13-14) but rather to serve Him. Discuss how this principle runs counter to the philosophy of the world today.

Family Singing

Christ, Whose Glory Fills the Skies (Trinity Hymnal #398); That Man Is Blessed (Psalter #1A)

Family Prayer

Thank the Lord for His faithfulness to you and your family by visiting you in Jesus Christ in order to redeem you. Ask Him to strengthen your thankful response to Him. Ask Him to make His duties a delight for you.

CHAPTER 4

The Savior Is Born

TODAY'S READING: LUKE 2:1-20.

Introduction

Today's passage is heard often around Christmas time and often wrongly gives a romanticized picture of Christ's birth. Today's passage, properly considered, shows us Christ's humiliation, even at His birth. But this humiliation allows the rest of the passage to focus on good news for the world.

Bible Teaching

To help break down the passage, we have divided this passage into three main sections:

◀ 2:1-7. This section addresses the historical setting, significant landmarks, and familial connections surrounding Christ's birth. Although seemingly peripheral issues regarding Christ's birth, they are significant in showing God's government of all His creatures and all their actions. From a Jewish perspective, all was lost. The nation was under the rule of the hated Caesar, and David's once-mighty line was laid low. However, it is exactly in that weakness that God sovereignly orchestrates the fulfillment of Micah 5:2. The mighty emperor of Rome is a simple puppet in the hands of God as He works out His plan of redemption, beginning humbly in a stable.

◀ 2:8-14. Jesus' arrival is not made in the halls of power but to shepherds at night. The humiliation of Christ's earthly ministry is emphasized in Luke's birth narrative, and yet there is already a hint of His heavenly glory. The connection to David, salvation, and His heavenly title of Christ, or Anointed One, show the divine purpose in His arrival: restoring peace between God and man. The angels appear to shepherds, a despised class at the time of Christ's birth, and proclaim the best news that will ever be heard. The announcement is climaxed with the 4th song about the Incarnation (v. 14). In it the angels sing praise to the Lord for the redemption He has sent in Jesus.

◀ 2:15-20. The shepherds show great faith in the words of the angels. They hear the message and hurry to see what was told to them (v. 16). With the angels' words confirmed in seeing the child, they praise God (v. 20). The angels declare the peace of the gospel in their announcements, and the shepherds take this message at face value.

Family Discussion

Today's lesson teaches us about the humiliation of Christ. However, instead of focusing exclusively on His suffering, this passage is connecting His affliction with the glory that will be His when His earthly ministry is complete.

Little Children: Talk to your children about what kings and queens are like. Show them how Jesus' birth is not what you would expect for a king. Point them to the song of the angels in v. 14 to show how God is still glorified in Jesus' birth.

Middle Children: Looking at Westminster Shorter Catechism #23 briefly talk about Christ's redemptive offices of prophet, priest, and king. Talk about His humiliation as part of His priestly work on our behalf. Show them His kingship established through passages such as Isaiah 9:6-7.

Older Children: Consider both the way the shepherds receive and respond to the message of the arrival of Christ. They receive the word of God in faith, and they respond by sharing the good news of the gospel. Does your family respond in the same way? What are the things we love to talk about? Why not the arrival of the Messiah?

Family Singing

Joy to the World! The Lord Is Come (Trinity Hymnal #195); Who with God Most High Finds Shelter (Psalter #91A)

Family Prayer

Thank the Lord for sending His Son into the world in humiliation that He might stand in our place. Ask God to grant your family the proper attitude in receiving the Word of God, but also the appropriate zeal in responding to His Word.

CHAPTER 5

The Savior Identified
TODAY'S READING: LUKE 2:21-38.

Introduction
There are times when we can identify someone's children just by looking at them. Their features and mannerisms betray their parentage. However, if we are wise, we will not assume their identity, in case we are wrong. To be certain, we ask for the child's name. In these verses Jesus' identity as Messiah is given, in a sense giving us His name.

Bible Teaching
When Jesus is presented in the temple there are three main events to consider:

◀ 2:21-24. Starting back in 2:21, the Bible shows Jesus meets all the Law's requirements. The One to be the sinless substitute has been born, and even as a baby He is submitted to the Law in His circumcision (v. 21). He is circumcised on the eighth day (Luke 2:21; cf. Lev. 12:3) and, as the firstborn son, He is redeemed (Luke 2:22; cf. Num. 18:15-16), submitting Himself to the shadows of the Mosaic Law. This obedience is crucial to His messianic office. He perfectly obeys all of God's Law in a way our first representative, Adam, did not. Even when unable to perform the obligations Himself because of His infancy, the Lord uses Joseph and Mary to accomplish His purpose. Four times in this section, verses 22, 23, 24, 27, and once in the next, verse 39, Luke highlights their obedience to God's Law.

◀ 2:25-35. The song of Simeon, or the Nunc Dimittis, marks the 5th song sung in response to the Incarnation. Simeon is a righteous man, meaning he desires to obey the Lord, not that he does so perfectly. He sings about the corporate benefit for God's people, whether Jew or Gentile, realized in the arrival of the Messiah. His heart is at peace now that he has seen God's promise fulfilled and the One who will fulfill it. Filled with the Holy Spirit, Simeon speaks the very words of God and announces the arrival of the second person, the Son. As Joseph and Mary marvel over his words, Simeon goes on to speak of the pivotal nature of Christ's life. His arrival results in falling or opposing in those hardened, and the rising of many in the converted.

24

◀ 2:36-38. Anna is unique in Scripture. First, she is a prophetess, an office usually reserved for men. Second, she was married for 7 years in her youth, then lived as a widow until her current age 84. As a widow she spent all her time at the temple worshiping, fasting, and praying. She is also present in the temple with Simeon, Mary, Joseph, and Jesus. She thanks God for Christ's arrival and announces Him to all in the temple.

Family Discussion

First, show that Jesus qualifies to be our Savior because He obeys all of God's Law from birth. Second, discuss how Scripture specifically names Him as such.

Little Children: Talk about sin as breaking God's Law (see Westminster Shorter Catechism #14). Take time to show that Jesus never disobeyed God's Law and, therefore, can be our Savior.

Middle Children: Talk about how family resemblances are not enough to make us sure about someone's identity. Show how only someone's name can give certainty. Show how the words of Simeon and Anna give this kind of certainty about Christ.

Older Children: In verse 34 Christ is predicted to cause the 'fall and rising of many...' Talk about Christ as the instrument of hardening and conversion among men. Discuss whether they are opposing Christ or through faith know they can die in peace.

Family Singing

Come, Thou Long-Expected Jesus (Trinity Hymnal #196); Why Do Gentile Nations Rage? (Psalter #2B)

Family Prayer

Thank the Lord for Christ's perfect obedience. Ask the Lord to grant you a joyful response to the account of His arrival.

CHAPTER 6

Fully Human

TODAY'S READING: LUKE 2:39-52.

Introduction

This account is about growing up but is quite different from typical coming-of-age stories. When describing childhood events, storytellers usually use life-shaping events. However, this account about Jesus is not intended to teach us how Jesus became who He is, but rather that He is fully human. He experienced life like any other person with a reasonable soul, which is important when it comes to His qualification to be our Great High Priest.

Bible Teaching

Glimpses into Jesus' childhood are scarce in the Gospels. However, in our passage we find two separate records about Jesus' youth:

◀ 2:39-40. Following the events in the temple, Jesus' parents return to their home town, Nazareth. Luke leaves out the flight to Egypt (cf. Matt. 2:13-23), but nothing in Luke's Gospel conflicts with Matthew's. Luke simply passes over that portion of Jesus' life because it was not relevant to his purposes. When Jesus returns to Nazareth, He grows and develops as any other Jewish child of His day. Physically, He grows in strength. Spiritually, as the Anointed One of God, He is filled with wisdom beyond His years because the favor of God rests on Him.

◀ 2:41-52. The piety of Joseph and Mary is seen in their religious habits. Each year they went up to the Passover feast, one of the three main feasts of the Israelites, the other two being the Feast of Weeks or Harvest and the Feast of Booths or Ingathering. The women and children were allowed, but not required, to attend these feasts (cf. Deut. 16:16), but Joseph and Mary regularly attended the feast together. This account probably records Jesus' first participation since He went up 'according to custom.' It was customary for twelve-year-old Jewish boys to observe the Passover celebration one time before they became a son under the Law (Bar Mitzvah) at age thirteen. During this trip to Jerusalem, Jesus, Joseph, and Mary become separated. The parents return home assuming He is among the company of friends and relatives returning to Nazareth. When they realize He is missing, they rush back to Jerusalem and find Him in the temple answering the priests' questions with astonishing clarity for a boy His age. Not only is He theologically astute, but He also already clearly knows that His true Father is God Himself. When they take Him home, His continued physical and spiritual growth is recorded. He grows in favor with God and man because His life was exemplary through the absence of sin.

Family Discussion

Use Hebrews 4:14-15 as a springboard to discuss the humanity of Christ and its importance.

Little Children: Ask your children for some ways they know Jesus was fully human. Help them by pointing to His birth in the manger.

Middle Children: Make the distinction between childishness and sin. Show how it is possible to make a mistake without sinning. Jesus could have gotten a math problem wrong or used the wrong nail when helping Joseph in his shop. Use this distinction to teach how Jesus could grow in wisdom. Also show the significance of Jesus' obedience to His parents.

Older Children: Examine the humanity of Christ. Talk about the significance of Jesus submitting to His parents as the Creator of all things. Discuss how Jesus could grow in favor with God and His astounding biblical knowledge. How do these things make them marvel at the Incarnation?

Family Singing

O the Deep, Deep Love of Jesus! (Trinity Hymnal #535); Why Do Gentile Nations Rage? (Psalter #2B)

Family Prayer

Ask the Lord to bless and increase your understanding of what it means that Christ became fully man. Thank Him for His love for you in sending His Son to be the Great High Priest.

CHAPTER 7

The Ministry of John

TODAY'S READING: LUKE 3:1-22.

Introduction

We live in a time of fleeting celebrity. People are famous one year and completely forgotten the next. Today's celebrity battles constantly to remain relevant. John the Baptist is different. He understands his main purpose is to point to Christ. He knows that his task is to be the herald announcing the Son of God has come to earth to stand in man's place.

Bible Teaching

Luke treats John's entire ministry in twenty-two verses, dividing his work into three parts:

◀ 3:1-6. Luke first records the context of John's ministry. Luke gives us our chronological bearings by noting the significant rulers of this time: the emperor (Tiberius Caesar), the governor (Pontius Pilate), and the tetrarchs (Herod Antipas and Phillip). This section shows Israel as defeated politically and off-center spiritually with two high priests serving, which is contrary to Scripture (cf. Exod. 29:29-30). In this unexpected context we see the fulfillment of Old Testament prophecy. Isaiah 40:3-5 speaks of the one who will announce the arrival of the promised Messiah. His birth actually points to Christ and His imminent arrival.

◀ 3:7-18. Luke gives a sampling of John's words spoken throughout his 6-12 month ministry. Clearly John is not the coddling type. He uses strong words to call people to repentance and to bear fruit. He specifically addresses two sins he sees in the land. First, he warns Israel about their complacency, which flowed from their presumption on God's favor because they were descendants of Abraham (vv. 8-9). Second, he warns people generally against the sin of greed, which is idolatry (cf. Col. 3:5). But in all his boldness and brashness John has one thing in mind: the glory of Christ. John understands the significance of the Savior's ministry, which will far exceed his.

◀ 3:19-22. John's message is not well received. John's message offends them, including the tetrarch Herod whom he confronts with immorality. Herod, a wicked man, further adds to his guilt by arresting John and effectively ending his ministry. John's ministry is short because its purpose is already accomplished. The Savior has come, therefore his fame must spread. The transition is finalized at Jesus' baptism, marking the beginning of His public ministry as priest of His people. The Trinity celebrate their plan of redemption with the Father's voice, the Spirit's descent, and the Son's human presence. Christ has come into the world to accomplish redemption.

Family Discussion

Discuss how the glory of Christ should be the center of our thoughts, words, and actions.

Little Children: Ask your children if they know what you really like to do. They will know either by watching you or hearing you tell them about it. Talk about the importance of showing our love for God by the things we do.

Middle Children: Talk to your children about John's willingness to be of no consequence in his service to the Lord. Talk about his contentment as being grounded in his understanding of the glory of Christ's ministry. How should understanding Christ and His ministry of reconciliation shape us and our attitudes?

Older Children: Talk about the presumption of the Jews in verses 8-9. Ask about different ways this attitude can be manifest in the Christian home too. Press your children to see if they are presuming on God's favor because of their baptism, church attendance, or other external conditions.

Family Singing

O Worship the King (Trinity Hymnal #2); My Portion Is the Lord (Psalter #119H)

Family Prayer

Pray for boldness in your obedience to God. Ask Him to strengthen your hearts against the temptations that are sure to come from the world, the flesh, and the devil. Thank Him for giving you new hearts that can will and work for His good pleasure.

CHAPTER 8

The Problem with Genealogies

TODAY'S READING: LUKE 3:23-38.

Introduction

The skeptic will turn to today's passage and declare the Bible is not true. They do so because the genealogy of Jesus found in Matthew 1:1-18 disagrees with Luke's. The names that Luke lists from Joseph to Zerubbabel (vv. 23-27) and Shealtiel to David (vv. 27-31) do not match with Matthew's. But this account actually builds our confidence in God's Word.

Bible Teaching

Some differences between Matthew's (cf. Matt. 1:1-18) and Luke's genealogies are insignificant. First, Matthew works from history to current times, whereas Luke works backwards. This difference is simply stylistic preference. Second, Matthew traces Jesus back to Abraham, while Luke goes back to Adam. Matthew writes to a Jewish audience and therefore connects Jesus to Abraham. Luke writes to the Gentile Theophilus and connects Jesus to all of mankind in Adam. The major objections, however, are usually reserved for the differences in names.

Thirty-nine names differ between the genealogies, but where the Bible critic cries 'Fraud!', the Christian does not. He may not have an answer that satisfies the critics, but that is not necessary. God has given us His Word, and we can trust it. Besides, there are plausible explanations for the differences between these genealogies.

◀ Explanation 1. Some hypothesize Joseph's mother had two husbands which would give Joseph an adopted and biological father. The differences in the genealogies are then explained by saying that one genealogy follows Joseph's biological father while the other his adopted father. This view was held by many early church fathers.

◀ Explanation 2. Some scholars suggest Matthew traces the legal descent of Jesus, or His tie to the throne, while Luke follows Jesus' natural descent or parentage. This idea suggests the Davidic line jumps branches in the family tree from Solomon to David's other son Nathan when Athaliah kills off

Ahaziah's sons in her coup (cf. 2 Kings 11:1). So the legal descent flowing from Solomon and the natural descent from Nathan account for the different names. Most pre-18th-century scholars held this view.

◀ Explanation 3. Most scholars today believe Matthew's genealogy is Joseph's line while Luke's is Mary's. The explanation is grammatical. Greek proper names can receive a definite article (for example, the John). All the names in Luke have a definite article except Joseph. This omission makes Joseph a parenthesis. The flow of the sentences in verse 23 is then thought to be 'being the son (as was supposed) of Joseph, [but really being] the [grand]son of Heli.' In extra-biblical sources, Mary is listed as the daughter of Heli.

These are possible explanations refuting the charge of a faulty Bible. The critic comes assuming fault, but the Christian should come assuming reliability.

Family Discussion
Take some time to discuss the faithfulness of God's Word.

Little Children: Teach your little children to trust the Bible. Ask them if they believe you when you make a promise to them. Teach them from 2 Timothy 3:16-17 that God's promises are always true.

Middle Children: Ask your children if they believe the car can get them where they need to go. Talk about their trust in the car despite not understanding exactly how it works. Talk about God's words as always being reliable (cf. 2 Tim. 3:16-17).

Older Children: Discuss this quote from Matthew Henry: 'It is well for us, that our salvation doth not depend upon our being able to solve all these difficulties...'[1] Discuss the assumption of the trustworthiness of God's Word.

Family Singing
How Firm a Foundation (Trinity Hymnal #94); Your Word's a Lamp (Psalter #119N)

Family Prayer
Thank God for the reliability of His Word. Pray for protection against doubt and help in delighting in His revelation.

---

1. Matthew Henry, *Matthew Henry's Commentary on the Whole Bible* (Grand Rapids, MI: Guardian Press: 1976), 356.

CHAPTER 9

The Temptations of Christ

TODAY'S READING: LUKE 4:1-13.

Introduction

If you want to test your young children, hide a camera in a room and, with the camera recording, give them two choices. They can either have the one piece of candy on the table now, or a lot of candy if they wait to eat until you come back. You will get years of enjoyment out of the footage. This experiment tempts them where they are weakest: candy. Satan tries this same strategy with Jesus, but Christ only desires to do His Father's bidding.

Bible Teaching

The account of the temptation of Jesus tells us when He is tempted, how He is tempted, and what happens after He is tempted:

◀ 4:1-2. Christ is tempted based on God's direction. Following His baptism, the Holy Spirit leads Jesus into the wilderness. There the devil tries to exploit His weakness. After forty days of fasting, the evil one thinks the moment is right and brings the full force of his tricks to tempt Jesus. Here is found one of the great understatements of Scripture when it says, 'he was hungry' after Jesus endures a forty-day fast.

◀ 4:3-13. Satan tempts Jesus three times. The first deals with Jesus' desires and may seem harmless. In Luke 9 Jesus feeds 5,000, so why not feed Himself here? But Satan tempts Jesus to follow His own desires, although He is in the wilderness at God's instruction. Jesus came to do His Father's will. The second temptation deals with authority. Satan takes the same approach as he did with Eve, trying to create envy toward worldly power within Jesus. Satan shows Jesus all the kingdoms of the world, promising them all to Him. But Satan's offer is deceitful because if Jesus accepted it He would be disqualified from being the substitute for God's people. In the third temptation, Satan twists Scripture to entice Christ to presume on God's favor. Although Jesus' ministry will end in His death, His laying himself down is not reckless, but intentional.

◀ This passage also emphasizes the distinction between Adam as man's first representative and Jesus as his second. In Eden, Adam, as head of the human race, does not withstand his temptations. He falls, plunging all of humanity into sin with him. After connecting Jesus to Adam in the genealogy, Luke now shows the beginning of the reversal of Adam's sin with the second Adam, Jesus (1 Cor. 15:45-49). Jesus withstands the temptations Adam and Eve could not, and so lays the foundation for His payment for the sins of His people.

Family Discussion

Lead your family in a discussion about the significance of Christ doing what Adam failed to do, to bring us life.

Little Children: Compare Adam's actions with those of Jesus. Show how Adam disobeyed God by eating the forbidden fruit in a garden filled with other fruit, while Jesus obeyed God even in the middle of great temptation in a wilderness.

Middle Children: Review the three ways in which Jesus was tempted. Show them the full obedience of Jesus in following His Father's desires. Talk about the significance of Christ's full obedience in light of a passage like 1 Peter 2:22-25.

Older Children: Discuss the necessity of Christ's sinless sacrifice. Look at Hebrews 4:15 and compare Christ, our Priest, with all the representatives that have gone before Him: Adam, Aaron, David, and others.

Family Singing

The Church's One Foundation (Trinity Hymnal #347); God Is Our Refuge and Our Strength (Psalter #46B)

Family Prayer

Ask the Lord to give your family the desire to seek first His kingdom and His righteousness. Ask Him to make you willing to deny yourself and able to resist the temptations of the world, the flesh, and the devil.

CHAPTER 10

They Love Him, They Love Him Not

TODAY'S READING: LUKE 4:14-30.

Introduction

Today's passage shows a remarkable shift. Jesus moves from the favored Son of Nazareth to a bitter enemy being run out of town. The change takes place when Jesus sets before them God's plan for redemption. Christ's expansion of redemption to include the Gentiles causes the people to become incensed. They turn from love to hatred in a matter of minutes.

Bible Teaching

To help see the cause for the change of mood in Nazareth, show man as in rebellion against God's glorious plan of redemption through faith for all kinds of people.

◀ 4:14-15. The special anointing of the Spirit on Jesus is recognized every-where. In that sense, the beginning of Christ's ministry is different from its end. First He is glorified by all, though people receive Him for their own purposes. At the end, they cry for His crucifixion because natural man hates God's gospel truth. Whatever the crowd's reaction, Jesus remains resolute to do His Father's will.

◀ 4:16-22. Jesus is in His home town Nazareth on the Sabbath and goes to the synagogue. When asked to read from the scroll, Jesus reads Isaiah 61:1-2, a prophecy dealing with the restoration of Israel. Jesus applies the prophecy to Himself, meaning the Spirit of the Lord is on *Him. He* is anointed to bring good news to the poor, to free captives, and to give sight to the blind. More importantly, *He* proclaims the Lord's favor. Jesus claims He ushers in the Jubilee, and the people in Nazareth love it. However, their love is selfish and they read their own meaning into Jesus' teaching. They desired to rid themselves of the Romans and return to national independence. Their reaction to Jesus' expansion of salvation to the Gentiles demonstrates the rebellion bound up in their hearts.

◀ 4:23-30. Jesus angers the crowd by mentioning two Old Testament miracles. First, during the reign of King Ahab, Elijah was sent to the widow of Zarephath (cf. 1 Kings 17:9). Second, Elisha heals the Syrian Naaman of his leprosy (cf. 2 Kings 5:1-14). Both Zarephath and Syria are Gentile lands. Jesus points out that God includes the Gentiles in the distribution of His favor. The people of Nazareth wanted God to favor Israel exclusively. A few minutes earlier Jesus was the favored Son, but now they intend to kill Him. They rebel against God's gracious promise and prefer their own plan.

Family Discussion

Take some time to discuss the glorious promise of the gospel seen in Jesus' inclusion of Jews and Gentiles together.

Little Children: Talk about Jesus' work as being for all the people of the world. Look together at Genesis 12:3 and see in God's promise to Abraham an inclusion of all the nations. Talk about God as the Maker of all kinds of people and how His love rests on people in all sorts of countries.

Middle Children: Looking at Genesis 12:3 and seeing the pervasive nature of God's plan of redemption, talk about the enmity that exists between the natural man and God. Talk about pride as the sin associated with rebellion against God. Show how man is so insignificant when compared with the God who works salvation for His people.

Older Children: Discuss how they can help each other recognize when they are following their own desires. Talk about the importance of knowing the splendor, holiness, and majesty of God when it comes to delighting in His plan of redemption rather than our own.

Family Singing

O for a Thousand Tongues to Sing (Trinity Hymnal #164); Bless the Lord, My Soul (Psalter #103B)

Family Prayer

Ask the Lord to help you delight in His glorious promise of salvation. Thank Him for including the Gentiles in this plan.

CHAPTER 11

Do Miracles Help?

TODAY'S READING: LUKE 4:31-44.

Introduction

Jesus' miracles are fascinating. Whether raising Lazarus, feeding the five thousand, or giving sight to the blind, these events grab Jesus' contemporaries' attention as they do ours when we read them. But the Bible was not written for entertainment. Luke writes his Gospel for the purpose of confirming what Theophilus was previously taught about God (cf. Luke 1:4).

Bible Teaching

This passage helps us rightly understand miracles by showing Jesus' divine nature and the purpose of His ministry.

◀ 4:31-42. At creation, God put a natural order in place by which He governs the processes of the world. For example, when matter is heated it expands, when cooled it contracts. This process continues undisturbed as God sustains the world He made and man is helpless to change these natural laws. However, what man is unable to do, God can do. When God interferes with the natural order of things the results are called miracles.

◀ In these verses, Luke records several miracles. These events were seen or felt by people, attributed to God alone, and validate the words of Jesus. But most significantly they tell us who Jesus is, and why He has come. In verse 33 the miracle of casting out a demon is recorded. Demons are not bound to obey men. But Jesus commands this unclean spirit with authority. The Creator of all things visible and invisible (see Col. 1:16) decrees and His creation must obey.

◀ In verse 38, Peter's mother-in-law is healed of her fever. Even in the most godly people, the effects of the fall are seen in illness. This woman is no exception. Yet Jesus is not ruled by natural processes as we are. He is God and can act outside the structures which would constrain man. Jesus is the Christ, and He rules over demons and has power over the effects of sin.

◀ 4:43-44. In verse 43, Jesus stresses His preaching as the central purpose of His ministry. The timeline of this teaching is important: first Jesus' words are rejected in Nazareth in verses 16-30, then He performs His miracles in verses 31-41, and lastly He reiterates the primacy of His preaching ministry. Jesus' words are the key. Miracles are not the agents of conversion. Jesus' words are. Jesus' miracles prove who He is, and His words instruct His hearers unto salvation.

Family Discussion

Talk about the centrality of God's Word over against experience, even experience as amazing as miracles.

Little Children: Talk about how Jesus' miracles show His power over demons and sickness. Ask them if they can make sick people better. Ask them if they understand what it means that Jesus can. Talk about what it means that Jesus is going to reverse the effects of the Fall by His death on the cross. How should that shape how they think, talk, and act?

Middle and Older Children: Who is Jesus shown to be by His miracles? Talk about the different elements of a miracle: sensible, attributed to God, validating the messenger's words. Show how it was important that Jesus' teaching was validated in light of His rejection at Nazareth (vv. 16-30).

Family Singing

A Mighty Fortress Is Our God (Trinity Hymnal #92); All, Like Mount Zion, Unmoved Shall Endure (Psalter #125)

Family Prayer

Thank the Lord for giving you the Bible to be able to know about salvation in Jesus Christ through Christ's victory over Satan. Ask to be filled with a love for His word that you would know what to believe about God and understand your joyful duty to Him.

CHAPTER 12

Called to Forsake

TODAY'S READING: LUKE 5:1-26.

Introduction

Winston Churchill was one of the greatest wartime leaders. The British people followed his rallying cries and sacrificed much in the process during World War II. But Christ's call is more important than Winston Churchill's. Christ promises us eternal salvation through His own blood, which is more important than anything.

Bible Teaching

Today's passage focuses on God's call and man's response. Christ's nature and His work cause a necessary response in those who trust in Him.

◀ 5:1-11. Jesus is teaching by the lake of Gennesaret or the Sea of Galilee. The crowd is so large that He asks Peter if He can preach from his boat. Following His teaching, Jesus the carpenter gives fishing tips to Peter, the fisherman. Were it not for what Peter knew of Jesus on account of the healing of his mother-in-law (4:38-39), Peter would have ignored Him. However, Peter listens and the resulting catch is astounding. Peter recognizes the significance: he has come face to face with God and declares himself unworthy of His favor. Despite Peter's reservations, Jesus still calls him to a unique task. Peter continues as a fisherman, but now he is God's instrument in fishing for the souls of men.

◀ 5:12-16. The healings of the leper and the paralytic teach about the compassion and mercy of Christ. Those most despised by society are precious in His sight. It is interesting to note man's response to the mercy of Christ. When properly understood and realized, the leper responds by commiting himself to a new obedience, following after the God who healed him despite his unworthiness. His actions prove his repentance.

◀ 5:17-26. In the healing of the paralytic, Jesus' words show what is truly at stake: the forgiveness of sins. More important than the healing of our body is the forgiveness of our sins. When Jesus tells the paralytic his sins are forgiven, there is an immediate reaction among the Jews. Only God is able to forgive sins, so Jesus makes Himself equal to God. To prove He is able to forgive sin He tells the man to get up and walk. Jesus asks His critics what is easier to say (v. 23). It would be easier to say his sins are forgiven because it cannot be verified. But Jesus proves His ability to forgive by healing the paralysis, which can be verified.

Family Discussion

Discuss the great impact an understanding of Christ's person and work will have on those who know Him, by talking about the reaction of the disciples, leper, and paralytic, and his friends.

Little Children: Ask if a sick person can make himself better. In the same way, help them see that only Jesus can heal their souls. Show how this gift is very precious. How can they show God that they are thankful for His gift?

Middle Children: Show the similarity between the physical condition of the leper and their spiritual state. The leper was physically unclean as they are spiritually. He suffers from an incurable terminal disease, and their souls are dead. When Jesus heals the leper, His cure is instant, as is the regeneration of their souls.

Older Children: 'We must allow no difficulties to check us, and no obstacle to keep us back from anything which is really for our spiritual good. Specially we must bear this in mind in the matter of regularly reading the Bible, hearing the Gospel, keeping the Sabbath holy, and private prayer.'[1] Discuss in combination with the teaching for the middle children.

Family Singing

Great King of Nations, Hear Our Prayer (Trinity Hymnal #713); O All You Nations of the Earth (Psalter #117A)

Family Prayer

Thank God for Christ and how He cleanses your soul from the guilt of sin.

---

1. J. C. Ryle, *Expository Commentary on the Gospel of Luke: Volume 1* (Carlisle, PA: Banner of Truth Trust, 1986), 142.

CHAPTER 13

Old Garments & Wineskins

TODAY'S READING: LUKE 5:27-39.

Introduction

When children choose teams, they usually select those who are most skilled first before moving to those who are least. The Pharisees present this same mentality. They seek to enter the presence of the God of heaven based on the strength of their works. However, when they lean on the strength of man, they are only leaning on a splintered staff. Christ's call isn't determined by human worth or contribution.

Bible Teaching

The inherent unworthiness of the disciples Christ calls is contrasted with the self-righteousness of the Pharisees.

◀ 5:27-32. Levi was a tax collector. In Jesus' day the tax collector was the worst kind of traitor. They were Jewish men who bid for districts where they would be licensed to tax their fellow Jews. In most cases, these collectors paid for their tax rights up front. In exchange they were given the might of the Roman sword to enforce their work. This arrangement was prone to much abuse. If people refused to pay their levied amount of taxes they were threatened with punishment. You can see how they would be shunned by their fellow countrymen. They were forbidden from testifying, receiving charitable gifts, and were ranked with prostitutes, robbers, murderers, and heathens. The Pharisees are incredulous about Jesus' willingness to associate with this despised class. Their disbelief stems from self-righteousness. They view the tax collector as a leper and declare him unclean next to their self-evaluated righteousness. They would never come to the Physician of their souls for healing next to the tax collector. But a man like Levi, who knows his desperate condition, comes to Christ by faith and is healed, in a spiritual sense.

◀ 5:33-39. The Pharisees continue to show themselves self-righteous and hypocritical. Their exclusive focus is on the external actions of man void of the love of God. Their motivation is gaining personal glory and enhancing their own reputation. They consider themselves more acceptable than Christ and

His disciples because they fast and pray. But what of the patched garments and the wineskins? The old garments and old wineskins represent the weakness of the disciples. They cannot do what the Pharisees are pressuring them to do without falling apart. To fast without the proper understanding of motivation would ruin them. They will fast (v. 35) but not until they are ready.

Family Discussion

Jesus' teaching helps you understand the proper context of our obedience. It is not a means to God's favor but flows from God's favor resting on you.

Little Children: Talk to them about tax collectors and how people did not like them. Discuss how they are like tax collectors before the Lord. Ask them if Levi changes how he lives and show them he does because Jesus calls him.

Middle Children: Use the example of fasting to show Jesus is not saying fasting is wrong. Explain how fasting for the wrong reasons is what is being attacked. Look at Daniel 9:3 and Acts 14:23 for examples of proper fasting. Talk about how they might fast as a result of God's love, not to earn His love.

Older Children: Look at Matthew 6:17-18 to see how the Pharisees fast selfishly. Look at Acts 13:2 and 14:23 to show how the disciples were not fasting for the approval of man. Talk about the beauty of fasting out of weakness to demonstrate your dependence on God rather than fasting in your strength as a way to show your righteousness.

Family Singing

The Church's One Foundation (Trinity Hymnal #347); My Portion Is the Lord (Psalter #119H)

Family Prayer

Ask the Lord to grant you humility and forgive you for your self-righteousness. Thank Him that Jesus is willing to have fellowship with sinners.

CHAPTER 14

Against Traditions, Not Laws

TODAY'S READING: LUKE 6:1-5.

Introduction

To understand what Jesus is saying in this passage, we must first study the biblical teaching on the Sabbath. Without it, we will interpret this passage from our cultural context, to our detriment. This background work will clarify that, rather than taking issue with the idea of Sabbath, Jesus attacks the Pharisees for imposing their non-biblical Sabbath traditions on others.

Bible Teaching

Studying the Sabbath principle will set the stage to properly study Jesus' teaching in these verses:

To understand the Sabbath we have to allow Scripture to interpret itself.

◀ The Old Testament shows God's institution of the Sabbath at Creation (cf. Gen. 2:1-3). God finishes His work and rests from the act of creating, not from sustaining it or working out His plan for redemption. In His rest He provides the world with a pattern of one day out of seven for rest. This rest is given for worship and forms a pattern for all ages. The Lord's worship is glorious rest, and the Sabbath is the weekly reminder of this blessing. This pattern is established even before Sinai's ceremonial laws are given and is therefore not abrogated by Christ. Therefore it is perpetually binding for all people. See Deuteronomy 4:13, Exodus 16:28-30, and Nehemiah 13:15-22.

◀ The New Testament shows the continuation of Sabbath-keeping. It is inferred in the Olivet Discourse, where Jesus predicts circumstances that will take place in A.D. 70. He speaks of destruction and encourages His hearers to pray their flight would not take place during the Sabbath (cf. Matt. 24:20). Notice Jesus fully expects the Sabbath to continue in A.D. 70. What is implied in Matthew 24 is stated explicitly in Hebrews 4:9 where the writer states there remains a Sabbath rest for the people of God. Both Testaments affirm the abiding nature of the Sabbath, because God's worship never ceases.

So then, Jesus is not taking issue with the fourth commandment but with the Pharisees' imposition of their applications on others. The fourth commandment calls us to remember this day of rest to the Lord by heeding two instructions: do not work and do not make anyone else work (cf. Exod. 20:8-11). Isaiah 58:13-14 adds the heart attitude to this command, teaching God's people to turn from their own pleasures and delight themselves in Him on the Sabbath. The Pharisees' reproof of Jesus' disciples is not founded on any of those precepts, but their tradition. Jesus tells them He is Lord of the Sabbath. Therefore He is its Master and their traditions are not.

Family Discussion

Examine your family's Sabbath practices and motivations.

Little Children: Talk about what it means to rest on the Sabbath. Show that they rest from daily work and not from all work. Talk about the joy of worshiping their Savior on the Lord's Day.

Middle Children: Examine what it means to obey the Sabbath by answering three questions about different activities: 1. Does it make me work?; 2. Does it make anyone else work?; 3. Am I delighting in the Lord? Ask these questions with regard to shopping, sports, visiting the sick, church, and family walks and other activities.

Older Children: Talk about neglect of the Sabbath as an attack on God's created order in Genesis 2:1-3. Talk about orienting yourselves properly toward the Sabbath. Instead of asking, 'What must I give up?' show the importance of asking 'What can I do to honor my Savior?' Ask if they view the Sabbath as a blessing from God.

Family Singing

Christ, Whose Glory Fills the Sky (Trinity Hymnal #398); Your Word's a Lamp (Psalter #119N)

Family Prayer

Pray that the Lord would help your family delight in the Lord's Day. Ask Him to help you to see its blessings.

CHAPTER 15

Carnal but Called

TODAY'S READING: LUKE 6:6-16.

Introduction

Your child's first temper tantrum is shocking. The child is on the floor, kicking and screaming, and you wonder, 'What happened?' Simply put, the child is manifesting his sin nature through his rebellion. This same nature is on display in this passage. The Pharisees' rebellion against God flows from who they are: children of the devil. And yet God calls rebels out of the world to be His disciples.

Bible Teaching

God calls us because of the act of His own perfect, unconstrained, sovereign choice, despite our wicked rebellion. First we will see the nature of man in the Pharisees and second Jesus' sovereign choice in His selecting the apostles:

◀ 6:6-11. The smoldering fire between the Pharisees and Jesus is beginning to burn more hotly. Ever since the healing of the paralytic (5:17), the Pharisees are suspicious of Him. They do not care about the truth of Jesus' words or goodness of His actions. They only care that He might violate their traditions, especially regarding the fourth commandment. But Jesus does not let tradition limit what He will or will not do on the Lord's Day. Their rebellion is clearly seen in their refusal to answer Jesus' question about lawful activities on the Sabbath (v. 9). They know the answer, but do not want to say. After the healing their response is even more telling: they want to kill Jesus (cf. Matt. 12:14). It is the natural reaction of Satan's offspring toward God. Love of God is love for Christ (cf. John 8:42-43), but hatred of Christ is hatred of God.

◀ 6:12-16. The Son's unique function in God's redemptive work is to do the Father's will (cf. John 6:38). To assist in this work, Jesus spends much time in prayer, even the whole night. Afterward, He chooses twelve men out of the larger group of His disciples. Jesus' choice is not dependent on a good resumé. These disciples will fail Him. Peter will deny he knows Jesus; Thomas will doubt His resurrection; James and John will lobby for political power. We may not understand why, but He most certainly did choose them. All people are like the disciples. Yet God in His mercy saves people. God chose Noah, Judah, Samson, and David, none of whom is a paragon of virtue. But God chose them to accomplish His purpose: to reveal His own glory.

Family Discussion

Help your children see man's sinful nature and God's merciful intervention. Show them Christ's desire to do all His Father's will.

Little Children: Ask them if they know what sin is. Teach them it is when they disobey God's commandments. Show them how everyone in your family sins. Show them that Jesus calls sinners to be His disciples despite their sin.

Middle Children: Talk about how, in verse 8, Jesus knows the thoughts of the Pharisees. Discuss His knowledge of the thoughts of the disciples too. Talk about what it means to come to Christ aware that He knows the depth of their sin.

Older Children: Talk about the unworthiness of Peter, James, and Thomas to be called disciples of Christ. Discuss how, since we are called by grace alone, being kept in Christ is not dependent on our works. For help you can consider Galatians 3:1-9.

Family Singing

O the Deep, Deep Love of Jesus (Trinity Hymnal #535); That Man Is Blessed (Psalter #1A)

Family Prayer

Thank God for setting apart some in the world to be His people. Ask God to bless you in your prayer life as individuals and as a family. Ask Him to give you strength to stand firm even if it should cost you.

CHAPTER 16

A Call to Self-Denial

TODAY'S READING: LUKE 6:17-36.

Introduction

In the Sermon on the Plain, Jesus preaches to the world, issuing a general call of the gospel. As He declares the good news, He teaches of the distinction between His followers and His enemies. Jesus calls His disciples to a life of self-denial flowing from the mercy of God in Christ, something entirely unfamiliar to His enemies.

Bible Teaching

The Sermon on the Plain seems to be a separate sermon from the Sermon on the Mount (cf. Matt. 5–7), The Beatitudes give us an understanding of the mercy of God in Christ. The verses that follow show how this mercy should cause great gratitude in us:

◀ 6:17-19. Besides Jesus' twelve disciples there is a 'great crowd of his disciples' in addition to a generic 'great multitude' that came to hear Him on this occasion. Jesus preaches to them all, proclaiming the call of the gospel into the world. Their illnesses are healed and demons cast out, further demonstrating and confirming His identity as the Anointed One from God.

◀ 6:20-26. Jesus begins the Sermon on the Plain with the Beatitudes. Beatitudes are simply statements promising great blessing. Jesus teaches His disciples that those who are poor, hungry, sorrowful, hated, and reviled are blessed. By studying the Beatitudes recorded in Matthew 5:2-12 we see that it is the spiritually poor, hungry, sorrowful, hated, and reviled who are blessed. It is the redeemed person's undying gratitude to Christ that makes him willing to forsake all for Him (v. 22). The poor are not, because of their poverty, more virtuous than the rich. Instead He is teaching that the disciple of Christ denies himself all things before he would forsake his Savior.

Jesus teaches the blessings of God, but also warns of woe. These threatenings are ominous. Jesus speaks of impending doom for those seeking their own pleasures; wealth, satisfaction, laughter, and prominence should not be our ultimate goals.

◀ 6:27-36. In addition to the blessings of living selflessly in response to Christ's mercy, Jesus also teaches consideration for the good of our neighbor. The golden rule (v. 31) is the summary of this principle: 'And as you wish that others would do to you, do so to them.' The world's instinct is to be favorable to those who treat them well. Christian disciples are instead called to selflessness. The motivation for obedience in the Christian life flows from God's charity to us when we were His enemies. Christ died for us while we were His enemies (cf. Rom. 5:10). Therefore, when we are selfless, it is the result, not the cause, of Christ's sacrifice for our sins.

Family Discussion
Focus on Christian self-denial in light of suffering these things on account of the Son of Man (v. 22).

Little Children: Help your little children see how they can deny self, such as sharing toys, clearing their dishes, etc. Connect these actions to how Christ gave Himself for them. Show them how Jesus denied Himself for their sake.

Middle Children: Talk about obedience to God flowing from salvation, but that it doesn't lead to salvation. Stress they should see their salvation accomplished by Christ and therefore serve Him joyfully in anything they might do.

Older Children: 'The people to whom our Lord says, "woe to you", are the very people whom the world admires, praises, and imitates. This is an awful fact. It ought to raise within us great searchings of heart.'[1] Discuss.

Family Singing
Come Thou Long Expected Jesus (Trinity Hymnal #196); Who With God Most High Finds Shelter (Psalter #91A)

Family Prayer
Pray to the Lord for strength to find your blessing in serving Christ at all costs. Ask for a love for the heavenly things.

---

1. J. C. Ryle, 179.

CHAPTER 17

Judging Rightly, Doing Rightly
TODAY'S READING: LUKE 6:37-49.

Introduction
Here we find some of the most misquoted Scripture in our day: 'Judge not, and you will not be judged.' However, by looking at its context notice that Christ is not teaching us to refrain from determining what is right or wrong. Instead He highlights God's position of Supreme Judge, with all men subject to His righteous decrees.

Bible Teaching
Before discussing the concept of living rightly it must be acknowledged that no one can properly do this. Since that is the case, every person should be primarily focused on their own sin, not the sin of their neighbor in this kind of study. In doing so, human judgment and strength are removed from the right living, or righteousness, so that all that remains is a hungry tree being fed by the root of the Holy Spirit.

◀ 6:37-42. In a world where God is rejected in many ways, common wisdom is that no one can assess another's morality. However, the Bible never presents such a view. Consider Paul's confrontation with Peter in Antioch 'because he stood condemned' (cf. Gal. 2:11-14). Paul condemns Peter's actions. But Paul's judgment has in mind God's pre-eminent authority over the world. He is the One who sets the standard (see also John 7:24). As the passage says, without Christ, man is by nature blind (v. 39), only a student imitating his teacher (v. 40). Man must recognize his own weakness and failings before God's righteous standard. Jesus never implies a person should not take the speck out of his brother's eye, but that he should do so while realizing he stands before the same Judge with his own sin.

◀ 6:43-45. The essential truth taught in these verses is that absolute good and evil exist. These are not defined by man, but by God. When God gives you a new heart and adopts you into His family, your thoughts, words, and actions *will* change. The fruit of your life, or your behavior, is a reflection of the condition of your heart. When the Holy Spirit takes up residence in your heart, you will most certainly bear His fruit.

48

◀ 6:46-49. This illustration shows you must look only to one place for your standards: Jesus' words. All of Scripture is the Word of Christ and therefore profitable for teaching, reproof, correction, and training in righteousness to equip the Christian disciple for every good work (cf. 2 Tim. 3:16-17). To live based on God's Word is the only sure foundation a man can have. To ignore the Word of the Lord is to have the same strength as a house built on sand.

Family Discussion

Consider how you are to live in evangelical obedience to God as your King.

Little Children: Teach your children what it means to obey God by looking at the commandments of the Bible. Talk about your inability to obey these commandments perfectly and your need for forgiveness through Jesus.

Middle Children: The commandments often tell the Christian what he is *not* to do. Look at the fruit of the Spirit (cf. Gal. 5:22-24) for positive instruction. Discuss how these fruits might take shape in your lives.

Older Children: This passage may make you question whether you are rotten because of your sin. However, repentance shows what kind of tree you are. A bad tree will not repent. Grief over sin actually shows the presence of the Spirit. Discuss in light of Romans 7:24.

Family Singing

Joy to the World, the Lord Is Come (Trinity Hymnal #195); All, Like Mount Zion, Unmoved Shall Endure (Psalter #125)

Family Prayer

Ask the Lord to keep you from self-righteousness. Ask Him to help you bear the right kind of fruit that flows from His Spirit.

CHAPTER 18

The Power of Jesus' Words

TODAY'S READING: LUKE 7:1-17.

Introduction

This account records tangible examples of the power of Christ's words. In these verses, Jesus speaks and a servant is healed and a widow's son restored to life. They clearly show that Jesus is God, speaking the very words of God. He is not *a* prophet, but *the* prophet. He comes in compassion and authority as the perfect fulfillment of God's covenant promise.

Bible Teaching

The first account shows Christ's divine nature through the power of His words. Who He is should affirm their trust and desire to build their house on this strong foundation. The second account confirms what is taught in the first.

◀ 7:1-10. In the account of the healing of the centurion's servant, the unexpected happens. As God's covenant people the Jews should have understood the trusted authority of the Messiah's words. Instead, it is the Gentile centurion who recognizes the authority of Jesus' words. The elders appeal for Jesus' help on the basis of the centurion's works. In their minds, his actions give authority to the centurion. They thought he should be helped because he loves their nation and built the synagogue (vv. 4-5). They have a horizontal perspective, expecting the centurion's works to command authority. However, the centurion does not expect his works to give him status but rather trusts the words of Christ as being authoritative (v. 6-8) because of who He is. When Jesus hears the message of the centurion (v. 9), He marvels. Even among the people of God His unique position is not recognized. The centurion appeals only for the gracious condescension of Almighty God. He knows he can come to God in no other way. This Gentile soldier has a proper, vertical understanding of God's dealings with man. Jesus identifies this perspective as faith.

◀ 7:11-17. When Jesus encounters a funeral procession leaving Nain, He addresses the woman with a seemingly insensitive exhortation not to weep. Although appearing cold at first blush, the words of Jesus actually comfort the weeping (cf. Luke 6:21). This unnamed widow is afflicted over her son, but when his death is vanquished, she is overwhelmed with joy. Christ's power to raise sinful men from death to life turns weeping to laughter. The raising of this man is a microcosm of the eternal condition of man's soul. People may weep in this life, but because of faith in the resurrection of Christ, there is laughter for God's people.

Family Discussion

Consider the authority of the words of Jesus as they flow from His person as God and man.

Little Children: Talk about what a prophet is. Help them to see he is someone who declares God's Word. Show how Jesus is uniquely qualified to proclaim God's Word and how His words can be trusted.

Middle Children: Look at the difference between the Jewish elders and the centurion. Show how the elders expected man's works to grant results, whereas the centurion trusted Christ as Almighty God. How might they be tempted to trust their own works for righteousness?

Older Children: Talk about the importance of approaching God in a spirit of humility. Talk about the appropriate posture in approaching God. Use Job 1:21 to show a proper understanding of God's authority. If needed, encourage your family to acknowledge your sin of self-righteousness, that the Lord might forgive you.

Family Singing

A Mighty Fortress Is Our God (Trinity Hymnal #92); God Is Our Refuge and Our Strength (Psalter #46B)

Family Prayer

Ask the Lord to guard your heart against relying on your own works. Ask Him to help you see your sin and recognize Christ's authority to vanquish it. Ask the Lord to give you laughter as you rest in the promise of eternal life.

CHAPTER 19

Man's Expectations, God's Intentions

TODAY'S READING: LUKE 7:18-35.

Introduction

Today's verses correct wrong understandings of who Jesus is. John must learn a painful lesson of not elevating his own expectations above Scripture's predictions regarding the Messiah. The crowd must learn that though John be a great man, they are to long for the Greatest who is not of this world.

Bible Teaching

We will look at this passage in two parts. First, there is the question of the disciples of John the Baptist, and second, the lesson using John as a picture of the greatness of man.

◀ 7:18-23. The Bible's saints are always portrayed honestly. Here, John the Baptist's weakness is shown. John was a great man, but he had his seasons of doubt with regard to who Jesus was. Doubt is different than unbelief. Unbelief rejects the truth, but doubt begs for clarification of the truth. John's expectation of the Messiah did not match what he saw. At one time he declared Jesus to be the 'Lamb of God, who takes away the sin of the world!' (cf. John 1:29). Now the imprisoned prophet sends messengers to confirm Jesus is the Messiah (v. 19). Having shown John's disciples that He fulfills Isaiah's prophecy ushering in the restoration of Israel (cf. Isa. 29:18; 35:5), Jesus corrects John's expectation. The unmistakable message is that Jesus is the promised Messiah. Nothing should distract God's people from his description of the person and work of Christ.

◀ 7:24-35. Once John's disciples depart, Jesus uses John to show the greatness of man is nothing compared to heavenly glory. Jesus describes John as the greatest man. He is determined (v. 24), rugged (v. 25), and the only prophet of his day to announce the Messiah's arrival (v. 26; cf. also Mal. 3:1; 4:5). Yet in contrast to him, even the least in the kingdom of God is greater. The crowds and tax collectors knew they were in need of such lifting up. However, the Pharisees did not understand, as seen in their refusal to undergo John's baptism of repentance. The Pharisees completely rejected

God. They preferred their own expectations with regard to man's salvation, which caused them to reject any conflicting teaching. Jesus' illustration proves His point. John the Baptist was too dour. He did not dance when they played the flute. But Jesus was too frivolous. They wanted Him to be more solemn (vv. 31-32). They did not recognize God's wisdom because they were busy looking at man through their own traditions. But God's children will recognize His wisdom (v. 35).

Family Discussion

Show that God is the only One to be followed and the graciousness of His person and work.

Little Children: Talk about the importance of entering into the kingdom of God by faith. Ask them what is more important: lots of toys, a big birthday party, or to be the least in the kingdom of God. How do you become such?

Middle Children: Talk about how easy it is to follow the opinions of men. Talk about the importance of seeking God's kingdom first (cf. Matt. 6:33). Also show Christ's graciousness toward the needy and how that should influence how we come to Him as needy creatures.

Older Children: Discuss the appeal of being famous and powerful. Discuss how Jesus' ministry was neither done from a position of riches and human power, or done exclusively for human riches or power. Why would this offend John the Baptist?

Family Singing

O Worship the King (Trinity Hymnal #2); Bless the Lord, My Soul (Psalter #103B)

Family Prayer

Ask the Lord to strengthen you in your love for Him. Ask Him to help you seek first His kingdom and His righteousness, knowing that all else will be given to you as well.

CHAPTER 20

Table Manners

Introduction

In our home we do not open birthday cards until our birthdays. Why? The anticipation elevates its value in the eyes of the recipient. The more we value a gift, the greater our joy when we receive it. So it is with the gift of salvation. When we realize the greatness of the gift of salvation, our joy and thanksgiving are deeper.

Bible Teaching

Luke teaches of the joy of salvation by comparing the gratitude of a sinful woman to a self-righteous Pharisee.

◀ 7:36-38. In today's culture, a meal is eaten around a rectangular table with straight-backed chairs. However, in Jesus' day food was eaten while reclining on couches around a large, low table. The guests would lie on their left side propped up with their elbow or a cushion. Their heads would be near the table and their feet would point away from it. People not invited to the dinner party could enter and observe the festivities, sitting along the outside walls. They would even talk with the guests. In this case the unusual event is not that univited guests are at the party, but that a woman of ill-repute enters the house of a 'righteous' Pharisee. Her love for her Savior compels her. She anoints Jesus' feet with perfume and wipes His feet with her hair to express her affection.

◀ 7:39-50. Her expression of love irks the Pharisee. He disdains the woman and Jesus: she is a great sinner, and He should know if He were a prophet. But what Simon the Pharisee mutters to himself (v. 39), Jesus addresses by way of illustration as if it was shouted from the rooftops. He tells a story about two debtors. One owes approximately US$40,000, the other one-tenth that amount. When both cannot repay, the moneylender cancels their debts. Jesus' question identifies the point: 'which of them will love him more?' (v. 42). The one forgiven more will love more. Jesus' point is that the woman's actions flow from her understanding of the greatness of what she has been forgiven. *Westminster Confession of Faith* teaches that our faith in God's promises is manifest in the yielding of obedience to His commands, trembling at His threatenings and embracing of the promises of God for life through accepting, receiving, resting on Christ's substitutionary sacrifice alone for justification, sanctification, and eternal life (*WCF* Chapter 14.2). Forgiveness comes through faith (v. 50); faith is accompanied by actions. In other words, the woman's faith is expressed in her action.

Family Discussion

Help your family see they have been forgiven much and, therefore, should love their Savior much.

Little Children: Talk about the most favorite present they could ever get. Ask them what they would do if you bought it for them. Show them how the forgiveness of our sins is far more valuable since our presents will break, but our forgiveness is eternal.

Middle Children: Talk about the temptation to despise other people for their sins while ignoring our own. How does this attitude demonstrate they think lightly of their sins? Talk about the importance of understanding the gravity of sin.

Older Children: J. C. Ryle said, 'The secret of being holy ourselves, is to know and feel that Christ has pardoned our sins.'[1] Discuss. Can you know facts about God's salvation and not be warmed in your heart toward Christ?

Family Singing

O for a Thousand Tongues to Sing (Trinity Hymnal #164); O All You Nations of the Earth (Psalter #117A)

Family Prayer

Pray for the forgiveness of your family's sins. Acknowledge how great they have been. Ask Him to help you to be humble and never despise others because we must all come to Christ in the same way: in true repentance.

---

1. J. C. Ryle, 238.

CHAPTER 21

What About God's Word?

TODAY'S READING: LUKE 8:1-21.

Introduction

In today's verses Jesus teaches about God's Word through seemingly unrelated accounts. However each account builds on the previous one. First, He issues a general call of the gospel. Second, in the parable of the soils He shows how man responds. Third, the lamp on a stand shows the reaction of those whose hearts are good soil. Finally, He shows the Christian's response as an evidence of his union with Christ. All of it flows from God's Word declared to man.

Bible Teaching

Each of the four sections mentioned above will be taken in turn.

◀ 8:1-3. As is Jesus' practice (cf. Mark 1:14-15), He declares the good news of the kingdom of God. This good news heralds the arrival of our perfect Passover Lamb (cf. 1 Cor. 5:7) to take away the guilt and dominion of sin. This kingdom is not God's universal reign over all things in this case. Jesus talks about this kingdom as something to be entered into (cf. Matt. 7:21; John 3:3). Jesus' kingdom is a spiritual kingdom entered by faith.

◀ 8:4-15. In the parable of the soils, Jesus shows the different responses to this gospel call. Jesus describes the meaning of the parable as secret (v. 10), not because its content is not known, but because its meaning is hidden. God must remove the veil from man's heart for him to see the truth (cf. 2 Cor 3:15). So Jesus describes four responses to the proclamation of the Word: first, complete rejection seen in the seed on the path; second, rejection because of testing represented in the seed on the rocks; third, rejection because of accumulating pressures pictured through the seed sown among thorns; and, fourth, acceptance displayed in the seed falling in the good soil.

◀ 8:16-18. Once the Word is received, those of good soil display it like a lamp on a lampstand. They cannot treat this glorious promise selfishly by concealing it. They desire to show others, and if they do not, it is evidence they are actually not good soil. In that case, whatever understanding they think they have, God takes away.

◀ 8:19-21. Just as the kingdom of God has no physical borders and therefore is entered by faith, so belonging to the family of believers is not marked by ancestry but by obedience to God's Word. Christ sows the seed. When the seed falls in good soil, the hearer puts the lamp on a lampstand, showing they are members of Jesus' family (v. 21).

Family Discussion
Discuss whether your relationship to God's Word is proper.

Little Children: Talk about the parable of the soils. Help them see the seed is the Word and talk about the different ways people respond to the Word. Teach them the importance of asking God to help them believe and trust His Word.

Middle Children: Make sure your children understand that they obey as evidence of salvation, not to earn it. Talk about the Bible as the declaration of the gospel. Talk about the good news of the kingdom from 1 Corinthians 5:7.

Older Children: Discuss the kingdom of God. Looking at John 3:3 and 5, discuss what is needed for citizenship in this kingdom. Talk about the present aspect of this kingdom seen in our current freedom from the guilt and dominion of sin. Also consider the future aspect of this kingdom which we anticipate at the second coming of Christ when the remains of sin will be forever vanquished.

Family Singing
O for a Thousand Tongues to Sing (Trinity Hymnal #164); My Portion Is the Lord (Psalter #119H)

Family Prayer
Pray that the Lord would continue to guide you into all righteousness and fruitfulness because of His Word.

CHAPTER 22

Actions That Speak

TODAY'S READING: LUKE 8:22-39.

Introduction

In these verses, Jesus performs two miracles, at the very least showing His special anointing as the Christ, or possibly displaying His divine nature. The demons and the people of the region see these powerful acts but reject Him. Only the disciples and the healed demoniac respond properly to the miracles.

Bible Teaching

Look at the two miracles to see Jesus as God's Anointed One, as His office is established by His command over nature and demons.

◀ 8:22-25. The first miracle is the calming of the stormy waters. It is important to connect this miracle with Genesis 1, another place where God speaks to creation with immediate effect. When God creates He speaks and the waters exist. So it is when Christ commands the waters in this miracle. Crossing the Sea of Galilee in a ship, the disciples are overwhelmed by a raging storm. They ask Jesus to help them, thinking they are about to drown. Jesus, asleep in the boat, arises, speaks to the water, and there is immediate calm (v. 24). The implication is not lost on the disciples who realize this calming of the seas was not normal. No other person could perform such a miracle (v. 25). Their question immediately reveals the purpose of the action: to show Jesus' power over creation.

◀ 8:26-39. The second miracle also shows God's power working through the Son, yet the response is different. A demon-possessed man meets them as they arrive in the region of the Gerasenes. Matthew 8:28ff says there are two men, but Luke talks about only one of them. The demon had so abused this man as to make him mad. He walked around naked, lived in tombs, and could not be contained by chains. So many demons tormented him that they identified themselves by the name Legion. Once the demons left the man and entered the pigs and drowned themselves in the waters, the herdsmen also recognized Jesus' abnormal power. They became afraid, but instead of drawing near to him they fled from His presence, returning only long enough to ask Him to depart. There was only one exception: the man who was healed. He asked if he could follow Christ. Herein we see the contrast between the kingdom of Satan and God. Satan's realm is one of destruction while entering God's kingdom brings peace to a tormented human soul. As in the declaration of God's Word, so in the witnessing of His miracles, there are those who worship in faith, and others who see yet reject.

Family Discussion

Discuss the importance of trusting the words and actions of Christ as being truthful because of His anointing.

Little Children: Put some water in a sink and slosh it around. Now command your children to tell the water to stop moving. Show them how people cannot command water to be still apart from God's power at work in them. Discuss how Jesus is a man but also God (cf. Gen. 1:1).

Middle Children: Talk about the different reactions to seeing the miracles. Look at Luke 16:31 for a further discussion on what it means to accept God's Word (and actions) with faith. Discuss how knowing things about Jesus is not enough, but there must be a corresponding trust in Him.

Older Children: Read Romans 1:18 together and discuss the response of the demons and people of the region. Talk about God as the Giver of faith (cf. Eph. 2:8-9). Discuss ways we can declare how much God has done for us.

Family Singing

Joy to the World, the Lord Is Come (Trinity Hymnal #195); O Lord, Our Lord (Psalter #8A)

Family Prayer

Ask the Lord to help you grow in your faith and keep you from doubt when you see Christ in Scripture.

CHAPTER 23

Faith and Healing
TODAY'S READING: LUKE 8:40-56.

Introduction
Jesus' power is clearly recorded in Luke's Gospel, yet people read of it and reject it as myth. They may have knowledge and even a sense of agreement about the Christian way of life, but they fail to entrust themselves to the only One who can save them. They have no saving faith.

Bible Teaching
In this section Jesus performs two miracles to be examined in turn:

◀ 8:40-48. While on His way to Jairus' house, a woman suffering from an illness for over twelve years interrupts His progress. This woman's flow of blood rendered her ceremonially unclean (cf. Lev. 15:25). This condition, therefore, had excluded her from the corporate worship of the people of Israel for over a decade. She had tried all sorts of cures (v. 43) but to no avail. When Jesus passes by, she comes up behind Him and touches His garment and she is immediately healed. By her simple action of touch, she entrusts herself and her healing into the hands of Jesus. Once power goes out from Jesus to heal her, He stops and waits for the woman to identify herself. As she comes forward in fear and trembling, she confesses the reason for coming to Christ. Jesus summarizes her report in His answer: her *faith* has made her well (v. 48). Much like the Israelites in the wilderness who looked at the bronze serpent for healing demonstrated their faith in God (cf. Num. 21:4-9), so also this woman's actions prove her faith in Jesus. Anyone who would draw near to Christ must do so in faith.

◀ 8:49-56. As Jesus finishes speaking with the woman, the report comes from Jairus' home that his daughter is dead. In response to the news, Jesus encourages the messenger to believe, perhaps a reminder of what has just transpired. Jesus can calm a storm (8:22-25), He can cast out a legion of demons (8:26-39), and He can heal a woman suffering from a chronic disease (8:43-48). The implication is that her death is not beyond His power either. Jairus must have faith and believe Christ is able to raise the dead (v. 50). He takes His closest disciples, Peter, James, and John, and enters the house. The people visiting the family laugh at Jesus when He says the girl is not dead. Jairus and his wife are exhorted to entrust themselves entirely to Jesus (v. 50). Again, anyone who would draw near to Christ must do so in faith.

Family Discussion

Consider the importance of faith in Jesus, the God-man. His word has been declared and His power displayed. Yet these things must be received in faith to be effective.

Little Children: Talk about what it means to 'believe in Jesus.' Talk about how Jesus makes their hearts alive by taking away their sins. Talk about what happens when they believe the works of Christ.

Middle Children: Talk about the woman expressing her faith in touching Jesus and compare it to Numbers 21:4-9. Also discuss the difference between the request of Jairus (v. 41) and the messengers who tell Jesus the girl died (v. 53). What did the woman and Jairus believe?

Older Children: Talk about faith as knowledge, agreement, and trust. First, they must know something about what or whom they place their faith in. Second, they must agree intellectually that this faith is justifiable. Third, they must entrust themselves wholeheartedly to the object of our faith. Look at James 2:19 to show the essential nature of the third component of our faith.

Family Singing

How Firm a Foundation (Trinity Hymnal #94); Bless the Lord, My Soul (Psalter #103B)

Family Prayer

Ask the Lord to increase your faith. Praise God for His Word and works.

CHAPTER 24

Who Is This Man?

TODAY'S READING: LUKE 9:1-17.

Introduction

Much that has preceded in Luke's Gospel serves to establish Jesus' identity through His power and might. His teachings and miracles build on each other to establish the good news of the kingdom of God and to reinforce what Theophilus was previously taught (cf. Luke 1:4). Today Luke puts the finishing touches on His case as He anticipates the eventual confession of Peter (v. 18).

Bible Teaching

Before moving to Peter's confession of Jesus as the Christ, Luke gives three more lessons.

◀ 9:1-6. When Jesus sends His disciples out with power over the demons, He shows the greatness of His authority. The power given by Jesus supports the disciples' preaching ministry (v. 2). Their ability to perform works in the spiritual realm simply confirms their preaching ministry. The disciples are called to preach the Word, and if it is rejected, they are to leave. The consequence of this rejection rests on the heads of those who turn away. Luke keeps building toward the question: Who is this man who can command such power?

◀ 9:7-9. King Herod, one of the chief villains of the Bible, also asks the question about Jesus' identity (v. 9). This king is not interested in Jesus as God's Son come in the flesh. This man, although moderately interested in spiritual things, was hopelessly disinterested in God's Word, works, and authority. He was the man who married his brother's wife and chopped off John the Baptist's head for confronting him about it. He hears the report and articulates the question: Who is this man about whom I am hearing such extraordinary accounts?

◀ 9:10-17. In feeding the five thousand, Jesus confirms His power one more time. After teaching the crowd all day, the disciples urge Jesus to send them to get food in the surrounding area. When the disciples respond with incredulity to Jesus' request to feed the crowd, Jesus tells the crowd to sit down. In their company they find five loaves of bread and two fish. Through them, Jesus feeds all the people. It is a miracle of creation. Jesus makes bread and fish appear out of nothing. In Deuteronomy 18:15 Moses tells the people of God to expect a prophet like him to come. Both Peter (Acts 3:22) and Stephen (Acts 7:37) apply this verse to Jesus: Jesus is the prophet like Moses. As God used Moses in the provision of manna in the desert (Exod. 16:12), so Jesus feeds His people. But Jesus manifests divine power, at the very least demonstrating His unique anointing as the Christ, but also showing something of His divine nature.

Family Discussion

Discuss Jesus' identity as being fully God and fully man.

Little Children: Briefly review some of the miracles and words of Jesus from the previous chapters of Luke. Talk about how Jesus shows His power over illness (5:12-15), sin (5:20), and death (7:11-17). Show how this means Jesus is uniquely the Chosen One, the Messiah.

Middle Children: Use Herod as an example of those who are curious about Jesus without any acceptance of His divine power. Talk about the difference between thinking Jesus is interesting and acknowledging Him as Redeemer.

Older Children: Look at Deuteronomy 18:15 and Moses as the prophet whom Jesus would follow. Show how the Lord provided manna in the desert, but how Jesus provides the crowds with the loaves and fish His disciples could not buy. Discuss Jesus' miracles and how they establish His superiority over the shadows of the Old Testament.

Family Singing

The Church's One Foundation (Trinity Hymnal #347); Who With God Most High Finds Shelter (Psalter #91A)

Family Prayer

Pray that God would make Himself known in the hearts of all the people in your family.

CHAPTER 25

Christian Self-Denial

TODAY'S READING: LUKE 9:18-27.

Introduction

The first three verses of today's passage are pivotal in the Gospels of Matthew, Mark, and Luke. They mark the point where a change in message and geographic orientation will characterize Jesus. Up to this point He declared the coming kingdom in Galilee, but following this passage He will begin to emphasize His suffering and the corresponding implications for His disciples.

Bible Teaching

Much of what Jesus has done so far points to His identity, but it has not been explicitly stated by His disciples. In the following sections the implications of Jesus' identity are treated, both for Christ and His followers:

◀ 9:18-20. Here is the first instance in Luke's Gospel where Jesus' disciples correctly articulate His identity. By this time, people had heard His sermons, processed His claims, and witnessed His miracles. Now Jesus asks His disciples if they have understood His message and miracles. Herod thought they might be explained by Jesus being Elijah or John the Baptist raised from the dead. The disciples begin by answering in the same way, based on what they have heard. However, Jesus wants to know what *they* think. Peter answers with confidence: the Christ, the Anointed of God. In his confession there is a proper recognition of the work of Jesus. He is sent from God and anointed to accomplish the work of redemption. However, Peter does not understand all that his answer means.

◀ 9:21-22. For the first time, Jesus gives a summary of His suffering to His disciples. Jesus will suffer, be rejected, and will die at the hands of the religious leaders. At the same time, the first glimmer of eternal hope is shown to the disciples. Jesus tells them He will also be raised after three days. The ultimate victory is predicted, but for now the focus is on Christ's suffering.

◀ 9:23-27. In talking to His disciples, Jesus does not give a typical 'feel-good' sermon. The picture of Christian suffering is very realistic and challenges those claiming to be His disciples to count the cost. If people decide to preserve their own lives instead, they will surrender the eternal for the temporary. Self-denial is evidence of the presence of the Spirit and an understanding of the unsurpassed treasure that Christ is. Failure to deny self indicates an ultimate love for self. To be joined with Christ is to live as He lived, and suffer as He did.

Family Discussion

Discuss the self-denial in the Christian life as it flows from an understanding of who Christ is.

Little Children: Give some examples of self-denial in different settings. For example, sharing toys versus failing to do so. Talk about the importance of their actions flowing from their understanding of Jesus' work for them.

Middle Children: Discuss Peter's confession in verse 20. Ask them if they believe in Jesus as God's Anointed Messiah. If they believe, what does that mean when it comes to their preferences? Whose do they choose, their own or the Lord's?

Older Children: 'We ought every day to crucify the flesh, to overcome the world, and to resist the devil.'[1] Discuss in light of Peter's confession in verse 20. Talk about the temptations to yield to their own desires and the disastrous eternal consequences that come with it.

Family Singing

Christ, Whose Glory Fills the Sky (Trinity Hymnal #398); My Portion Is the Lord (Psalter #119H)

Family Prayer

Ask the Lord to strengthen you to deny yourself as you are joined with Christ. Pray that the persecuted church especially would join Him in His suffering and glory. Pray that you would resist temptation.

---

1. J. C. Ryle, 309.

CHAPTER 26

The Majesty of God the Son

TODAY'S READING: LUKE 9:28-43A.

Introduction

In these verses the majesty of God is seen in Christ. In the Transfiguration three disciples, Peter, James, and John, see the Son in all His glory. These men, out of all of humanity, were given a unique encounter with the glory and majesty of God. However, their extraordinary experience is not the only way God's majesty is revealed. It can also be seen in the miracles of Jesus.

Bible Teaching

To show the majesty of God in Jesus, Luke tells two accounts. The first shows His glory in the Transfiguration. The second shows His majesty through the healing of a boy with an unclean spirit:

◀ 9:28-36. In this first account, the heavenly glory of the Son is seen when the veil of His flesh is lifted for a brief moment. Peter, James, and John, the innermost circle of Jesus' disciples, see His heavenly glory in a way no other people in history have. In the Transfiguration the three men observe Moses and Elijah talking with Jesus. It seems likely Moses signifies the Law and Elijah the Prophets, the very writings Jesus comes to fulfill (cf. Luke 24:27). When the cloud hides Jesus, the disciples hear the approving voice of the Father declaring His love for His Son. This same voice was heard at Jesus' baptism (Luke 3:22), yet the instruction to listen to Him is new. After the Father's voice is heard, the cloud is lifted and Jesus and the disciples are alone on the mountain. The Law and the Prophets make way for the One of whom they speak.

◀ 9:37-43. Although the Transfiguration was a powerful and unique event, the majesty and glory of Christ are also manifest in other ways. Following the mountain experience, crowds surround Jesus again and He shows them His majesty as well, though He is veiled in human flesh. The man who brings his son to Jesus for healing (v. 38) has already asked the other disciples to help him, but they were not able. However, Jesus only needs to rebuke the spirit to return the boy to his father in good health. The crowd was 'astonished at the majesty of God' (v. 43). Although Jesus' physical appearance is not altered in this case, His divine majesty is still clearly seen in His power. The majesty of God was made known to the crowd, yet it was not recognized.

Family Discussion
Talk about the majesty of God seen in Jesus and what appropriate responses might be.

Little Children: Talk about majesty from the perspective of a king or a princess. Talk about how you would behave before a king or president. Discuss how God is greater than any person, and they should respect and humble themselves before Him all the more.

Middle Children: Talk about how Jesus shows God's majesty not only in the Transfiguration but also in the working of miracles. Demonstrate how Jesus' power to heal, and even raise from the dead, shows the majesty of God because only He is able to do these things.

Older Children: In the parallel passage in Mark 9:6, the disciples are described as terrified in Jesus' presence. See also Ezekiel 1:28; Daniel 8:17; and Revelation 1:17. Discuss the fear of God in man when they see His majesty. Show how it flows from our knowledge of our sin (cf. Gen. 3:8).

Family Singing
Come Thou Long Expected Jesus (Trinity Hymnal #196); Who with God Most High Finds Shelter (Psalter #91A)

Family Prayer
Pray for God to impress His majesty on your family as revealed in the pages of Scripture. Praise the Lord together and recognize His glory, honor, power, and dominion.

CHAPTER 27

Not Earthly Power

TODAY'S READING: LUKE 9:43B-62.

Introduction

After the splendor of the Transfiguration and miraculous healings that have preceded, today's passage paints a stark contrast. As the disciples are still basking in what they saw, Jesus reminds them of what He is to suffer. Jesus predicts His own rejection and Luke foreshadows the world turning its back on its Creator.

Bible Teaching

Jesus not only predicts the climax of His own humiliation in His crucifixion and death, but He also takes time to teach that the lives of Jesus' disciples will be marked by suffering and deprivations:

◀ 9:43b-45. To protect the disciples from losing track of His ministry objective, Jesus reminds them He did not come to establish temporary glory on the earth. He came to purchase heavenly glory for those who place their faith in Him. In order to point the disciples toward that truth, Jesus removes their false expectations. Jesus came to die. At this point, the disciples are not granted the wisdom to discern the meaning of this statement.

◀ 9:46-56. Despite Jesus' reminder about His suffering, the disciples are focused on establishing Jesus' glory on earth. The disciples begin to dispute their own comparative importance (vv. 46-48). Jesus uses a child to show the folly of such thinking. Children were regarded as among the least significant members of society. However, Jesus urges His disciples not to be concerned with those who are influential, but rather to receive the insignificant. Jesus' disciples are called to be servants. But John's response in verses 49-50 shows his ignorance. He has just been told to think less of himself, but he finds someone whom he can disparage and look down on. Jesus patiently corrects him. Finally, in verses 51-56, the disciples want to call down fire from heaven on those who do not receive Jesus. The disciples are again seeking to preserve Christ's earthly glory as they thought it should be established: a this-worldly, physical, political kingdom.

◀ 9:57-62. Finally Jesus addresses the root sin beneath the would-be disciples' intentions. They are craving the glory of an earthly kingdom. However, Jesus shows that the comforts of this life are nothing for the follower of Christ. Neither home, nor family, nor friends have primary claim on the Christian. His work is only for his King, to go and proclaim His heavenly kingdom.

Family Discussion

Help your family see that since they are promised heavenly glory they can cheerfully forego earthly glory.

Little Children: Ask your children to name the most precious thing they can imagine. Talk about how Jesus is more precious than what they mentioned. Talk about Jesus as the greatest gift and treasure anyone could ever have. Should they ever give this treasure up?

Middle Children: Of course your children love their family and friends, but what happens if they are pressuring or leading them to forsake Christ? Talk about the importance of making Jesus the One they follow first. Discuss what kinds of things they must be willing to give up to follow Christ.

Older Children: Talk about the misunderstanding of the disciples in placing the earthly above the heavenly. Discuss how they are like the disciples. How do they violate the principle in verse 48? Should there be a celebrity culture in the church of Christ? Who is only the proper celebrity in the church of Christ?

Family Singing

O Worship the King (Trinity Hymnal #2); Your Word's a Lamp (Psalter #119N)

Family Prayer

Ask God to help you be willing to surrender everything to follow Christ. Pray that the Lord would help us to see Jesus' glory in our weakness.

CHAPTER 28

Travel Stories

Introduction

The sending out of the seventy-two disciples shows the focus and safety of the Christian. Jesus sends the disciples to teach, heal, and declare the arrival of the kingdom of God. Though Jesus sends His disciples out knowing they will be rejected in places, He knows there is great blessing in carrying out this charge as long as the disciples hold firm to Christ.

Bible Teaching

Today's verses are divided between the instruction given by Jesus and the experience of the disciples:

◀ 10:1-16. When Jesus sends His disciples out there are several noteworthy observations to make. First, Jesus sends them out completely dependent on the Lord's provision. They do not leave equipped with money, clothing, or friends. Second, their mission is to proclaim the good news and heal the sick. The latter demonstrates the validity and power of the former. The disciples are sent out as Christ's ambassadors, and are tasked to declare the same message Christ does. In that sense, a rejection of their message is a rejection of His (v. 16). A rejection of Christ's message means final judgment more severe than what Sodom received when they were judged.

As if anticipating the rejection, Jesus pronounces woe over Chorazin, Bethsaida, Tyre, Sidon, and Capernaum. Tyre and Sidon were Gentile cities of commerce along the Mediterranean Sea. However, Chorazin, Bethsaida, and Capernaum were Jewish cities likely even frequented by Jesus as part of His itinerant preaching ministry. Whether by the tribes of Israel or Gentile outsiders, the Word of Christ is rejected at their eternal peril. The greater the knowledge of the hearer, the less bearable the judgment on that person will be.

◀ 10:17-20. Jesus tempers His disciples' enthusiasm following their successes. They have returned ecstatic about their power over demons in Christ's name. However, Jesus shows them these things are possible because of the Lord's working to hold back the evil one (v. 19). He teaches them that rejoicing over the heavenly inclusion of their names, demonstrated in their serving their King in His kingdom, should be their priority instead. The casting out of demons is simply a manifestation of the work of God in them.

◀ 10:21-24. In His prayer, Jesus thanks the Father for His mercy to weak vessels. Christ's disciples are not powerful men and women. They do not come to God in the power of the works of their own will, but rather through the sovereign blessing of the Father through the Son. They are like children, not wise, strong, or impressive. Yet God reveals the mysteries of salvation to them and through them.

Family Discussion
Focus on the central joys and blessings of being in Christ.

Little Children: Ask your children who is stronger: mom/dad or them. Help them to see that it is not physical strength that is important when it comes to loving Jesus. Rather it is the blessing given by God to see the salvation offered by Jesus.

Middle Children: Relate the disciples' lack of provisions for their journey to their inability to accomplish their mission. Show how God provided for their physical needs and granted them the spiritual power to accomplish the healings and casting out of demons.

Older Children: Talk about the significance of repentance from sin in the believer (v. 13) in light of the destruction pronounced over the cities. Talk about repentance as a gift from God given to those who are weak in their sin. What part does intelligence play in salvation?

Family Singing
O the Deep, Deep Love of Jesus (Trinity Hymnal #535); Why Do Gentile Nations Rage (Psalter #2B)

Family Prayer
Pray that God would make you childlike in your reception of the promise of salvation.

CHAPTER 29

Loving God with All Your Heart

TODAY'S READING: LUKE 10:25-42.

Introduction

The priority of the Christian's love for God is addressed in the first commandment: 'You shall have no other gods before me' (Exod. 20:3). This word 'before' is saying you may have no other gods in the Lord's presence. To entertain any other gods is to pervert right love for Him. Jesus teaches His disciples that God must be the center of what they say, do, and think.

Bible Teaching

These verses can be divided up by first looking at the parable of the Good Samaritan and then the account about Mary and Martha.

◀ 10:25-37. A lawyer tests Jesus about how to inherit eternal life. When Jesus directs the man to the Law, He combines Deuteronomy 6:5 and Leviticus 19:18. In Deuteronomy, God calls His people to love Him and, in Leviticus, to love their neighbors. These verses are a summary of the Ten Commandments. The first four teach how to love God, and the last six our neighbor. God's people obey these laws in light of salvation given to them. But the lawyer is trying to obey them to earn salvation. His solution to his inability to keep the Law is to find a way to circumvent it (v. 29). Jesus instructs him with the parable of the Good Samaritan.

The parable is simple. The priest and Levite pass by the injured man, but the Samaritan cares for him. The Samaritan, hated by the Jews (cf. John 4:9), proves to be a neighbor through his mercy (v. 37). The lawyer wants to redefine what a neighbor is in order to justify himself, yet Jesus makes clear what it means to love his neighbor. To love his neighbor is to serve him out of love for God, and he cannot love God according to his preferences. He must follow God's description of how He is to be loved as laid out in His commandments (cf. John 14:21).

◀ 10:38-42. Obedience to God should be an expression of the heart's affections. Mary and Martha serve as a picture for us. Martha is hard at work, but does not labor out of love for Christ. Her service is a bleak duty, at least on this occasion, as can be seen in her resentment (v. 40). Mary's action is far more loving toward Christ. This passage is not teaching whether it is better to listen than to serve, rather it calls us to delight ourselves in Christ first, using every circumstance to demonstrate this joy.

Family Discussion

Examine yourselves as to what motivates your family's service to the Lord.

Little Children: Discuss how they obey God because He has saved them, not so that He will save them. Show them royalty acts according to their title. They do not become royalty by acting as one. Christians also act a certain way because of what they are: Christians.

Middle Children: Look at the summary of the Law: to love God and your neighbor. Talk about how love for their neighbor flows out of their love for God. Show how loving things or people can actually be self-serving.

Older Children: Talk about how Jesus' calling the lawyer to obey the Law was a way to bring him back to the first commandment. Talk about the Christian's striving to obedience as being different than works-righteousness. When Paul cries out in Romans 7:24, is he upset over God's call to obedience or his failure to obey God's Law?

Family Singing

O for a Thousand Tongues to Sing (Trinity Hymnal #164); God Is Our Refuge and Our Strength (Psalter #46B)

Family Prayer

Ask the Lord to help you, by His Spirit, to love Him with all your heart, soul, strength, and mind, and your neighbor as yourself.

CHAPTER 30

How to Pray

TODAY'S READING: LUKE 11:1-13.

Introduction

Prayer is an essential part of the Christian life, because it expresses our dependence on God. However, it is also one of the most difficult Christian disciplines to carry out consistently. The disciples face this same struggle, so they ask Jesus to teach them how to pray. Not only does He give them a form of prayer, but He also teaches persistence and diligence in prayer.

Bible Teaching

This chapter will first look at the Lord's Prayer and then at the necessary persistence in prayer to the Lord.

◀ 11:1-4. When Jesus teaches His disciples to pray this prayer, He does not mean it to be repeated verbatim. There are many other prayers Jesus offers (eg. the High Priestly Prayer in John 17). The point is to learn a pattern of prayer.

When praying that the Father's name would be hallowed, you ask that God would enable you to glorify Him. That means in your prayer you ask God to reveal or make clearer His glory in and through your thoughts, words, and actions.

When you pray, 'Your kingdom come,' you ask God to establish His rule in your life and the world. You are His kingdom's subject and are at war with Satan's kingdom. You are asking your King to preserve you as His subject, but you also want His eternal kingdom to be established in the world, at which time the imperfection of sin will be eternally removed.

When you pray, 'Give us each day our daily bread,' you acknowledge God provides all your needs. You ask to receive the comforts of this life. Notice, this petition is the first that asks for something for man. Notice, this petition is the first that asks something for ourselves.

When you pray, 'forgive us our sins,' you express your dependence on God for salvation. As God's creature, you offend God with your premeditated rebellion against Him as well as your thoughtless neglect of His Word. In prayer it is appropriate to acknowledge your sinful weakness and ask Him to remember His steadfast love. At the same time, you are to forgive others as Christ forgave you (cf. Col. 3:13).

When you pray, 'lead us not into temptation,' you recognize God's power to protect you from temptation but also to provide a way of escape when temptation comes (cf. 1 Cor. 10:13).

◀ 11:5-13. In this parable, Jesus teaches persistence in prayer. God desires to hear the prayers of His children, yet often they neglect it. Here Christ teaches they are to diligently lift up their prayers to God. He uses an argument from lesser to greater. If sinful man gives to a persistent friend or provides good things to his children, how much more will God give His children the greatest gift: the Holy Spirit?

Family Discussion
Talk about the importance of prayer as an acknowledgment of your understanding of God.

Little Children: Talk about different parts of prayer that do not involve asking God for anything. Talk about how you can adore God in prayer, confess your sins to Him, and give Him thanks.

Middle Children: Talk about the petitions in the prayer Jesus teaches. How can they be expressed in prayer to God? Give some examples of each and learn what it means to pray in the form of the prayer, not just using the prayer verbatim.

Older Children: Talk about James 1:5-8 and how it informs this passage about prayer. Talk about the common emphasis on supplications or requests in our prayers. Stress the significance of adoration, confession, and thanksgiving in prayer.

Family Singing
A Mighty Fortress Is Our God (Trinity Hymnal #92); All, Like Mount Zion, Unmoved Shall Endure (Psalter #125)

Family Prayer
Pray the Lord's Prayer together.

CHAPTER 31

Picking Sides

TODAY'S READING: LUKE 11:14-28.

Introduction

Jesus did many miracles, including casting out demons. Many witnesses of these acts marveled at His power, while others were hardened in their sin and tried to use His miracles as an occasion to speak evil of Him. However, Jesus' miracles actually prove His authority and demand obedience to Him.

Bible Teaching

This section can be divided into the casting out of the demon, the accusation against Jesus, and His corrective instruction in response:

◀ 11:14. Here, not in any chronological context, Luke describes Jesus' casting out of a demon. Very little is described about this event. The only thing we know is that the demon caused muteness, and Jesus cast him out. In response most of the people marveled as they witnessed something supernatural.

◀ 11:15-16. Despite Jesus' obvious divine power displayed, some tried to use this miracle to belittle Him. Some in the crowd claimed that Jesus must be the prince of demons to cast out demons. Others despised His miracle, looking instead for more spectacle from Him. Like the seed that fell on the path, nothing Christ would have done in their presence would have satisfied their carnal curiosities.

◀ 11:17-28. Jesus responds to their charges by appealing to Geopolitics 101. If any army turns on itself, it cannot mount a successful attack against anyone. Instead, armies attack foreign armies. Such is the relationship between Christ and Beelzebub. The domain of darkness is under attack by the kingdom of God. Christ is waging war against the prince of the power of the air.

In verses 24-26, Jesus shows there is no neutral army in this warfare. Once the evil is removed from a human soul it must be replaced with good. One must declare allegiance to his new King. Instead of worshiping the creature, man is called to worship the Creator. If he fails to do so, he is warned that his final plight will be more desperate than his original condition.

Finally, in verses 27-28 Jesus shows that what flows from His casting out of demons is not simply adoration over what He has accomplished. He points, yet again, to the balance of hearing and doing God's Word. Jesus shows that the Christian life is not one of simple appreciation, but of worship. We hear what God says, and we respond in action. It is in this obedience that the true blessing of God will be established because it is a sign of the indwelling of His Spirit.

Family Discussion

Today recognize the hostility between Jesus and the devil. Show how Christ's victory should result in joyful, obedient worship.

Little Children: Talk about what would happen on a team if a player took the ball away from his own teammates and shot at his own goal. Use this example to show how Jesus would not cast out demons if he was a demon. Talk about Christ as King and at war with Satan's kingdom.

Middle Children: Talk about how it is not possible to be a neutral party in the battle between the devil and Jesus. Discuss how not worshiping God is a hostile action against Him. Looking at Romans 12:1-2, talk about all of life as worship.

Older Children: Talk about how hearing and doing (v. 28) is preferred to a biological relation to Christ (v. 27). Review Ephesians 2:8-10 again to show your complete dependence on God for salvation. Talk about obedience as a fruit of salvation, not the root of salvation.

Family Singing

Great King of Nations, Hear our Prayer (Trinity Hymnal #713); That Man Is Blessed (Psalter #1A)

Family Prayer

Thank God for His power and the coming of His kingdom. Ask that His kingdom would be expanded through your family's testimony.

CHAPTER 32

Woe to the Pharisees

Introduction

Jesus is well known for His criticism of the Pharisees. Jesus speaks out against them because their teaching is dangerous. To follow them is to deny faith in God and His plan of redemption. The Pharisees trusted in their own actions to save. They denied the exclusive glory and majesty of God in salvation.

Bible Teaching

Jesus condemns the crowd through the sign of Jonah: as Jonah was in the belly of the fish for three days, so Jesus will be in the grave. Yet Jesus' generation prefers other lesser signs, leading Jesus to pronounce a series of woes on them.

◀ 11:29-36. Jesus' teaching is rooted in 11:16 where some reject His healing of the demon-possessed man, asking instead for a 'sign from heaven' (v. 16). Having not responded to them at first, Jesus now addresses their desire for the sensational. Instead of trusting the very signs already shown them, these thrill-seekers ask for something new. Their desire is not that they might understand, but rather that their appetites for the spectacular would be satisfied. Therefore, the only sign Jesus will give is the sign of Jonah. From Matthew 12:39-41 we know this reference points to the three days Jesus will spend in the grave. The whole purpose is to condemn the people for not looking to Christ as Mediator and Redeemer. When Jesus calls people to put the light on a stand and be filled with it (vv. 33-34), He is calling them to look to Him. To look to Jesus is to look to the light (cf. John 1:9), but if their eye is fixed on the wrong thing, they will dwell in darkness.

◀ 11:37-54. The Pharisees continually prove they dwell in darkness through their preoccupation with works as a justifying agent. In verse 38 ceremonial hand-washing is the stumbling block for the Pharisee. He cannot see the Savior on account of his tradition. He desires to see a man wash his hands, rather than serve God. To correct this error Jesus pronounces a series of woes. He focuses primarily on their emphasis on external compliance, rather than on love for God.

The lawyers take offense at Jesus' words. But Jesus has no patience for those who would rely on their works for justification. These teachings led to the death of the prophets and burdened their pupils. Jesus' words strike at the pride of the Pharisees, and they begin to try to think of a way to destroy Him. They begin with trying to discredit Him, tripping Him up with difficult questions.

Family Discussion

Talk about the importance of justification by faith alone.

Little Children: Talk about standing before a judge. When someone stands before the judge, he is not there for the laws he kept, but the laws he broke. So man is judged for his sin, not his 'good works.' Talk about Christ as their substitute.

Middle Children: Talk about the problem of asking for a sign. Show how the people did not really want to be convinced about Jesus but wanted to see a spectacle. Talk about Jesus as their Savior, not their entertainer.

Older Children: Look at the woes pronounced on the Pharisees and lawyers. See how their focus is on the external at the expense of the internal. Look at verse 42 to see whether or not actions are important. Talk about the proper motivation for obedience flowing from our understanding of His promises.

Family Singing

O the Deep, Deep Love of Jesus (Trinity Hymnal #535); O All You Nations of the Earth (Psalter #117A)

Family Prayer

Ask the Lord to forgive you for your hypocrisy and desire to earn salvation through works.

CHAPTER 33

What or Whom to Seek First

TODAY'S READING: LUKE 12:1-12.

Introduction

The life of man is not primarily lived out in front of people, but in front of the Lord. He sees all our thoughts, words, and actions and will judge us accordingly. Yet He is a merciful God, One who sends His Spirit to preserve His people even in the most difficult circumstances.

Bible Teaching

A person's true beliefs will be manifest through his actions. This passage addresses the hypocrisy of the Pharisees, points the reader to fear and serve God, and shows the significance of the work of the Holy Spirit in this process.

◀ 12:1-3. Despite the Pharisees' work to discredit Jesus, His popularity grows. As He teaches on the Pharisees' hypocrisy, He addresses the hidden, true motives of the Pharisee, which are not the glory and praise of God. Their external allegiance to God through their false piety will ultimately prove to be temporary only. One day all their secret sins will be made known (v. 2). In some cases this judgment will be executed swiftly, as in the case of Ananias and Sapphira (cf. Acts 5:1-11). In other cases the uncovering of hypocrisy will be revealed only at the end.

◀ 12:4-7. Christ directs the disciples toward their Eternal Judge. Instead of fearing man, Jesus calls men to fear God. God can condemn us to an eternity of suffering in hell (v. 5), but man's scorn will last eighty years at most. Only a fool would crave the approval of men at the expense of the splendor of heaven. Though man may have temporary control over your comforts, it is our faith in the Lord that keeps us from eternal suffering.

◀ 12:8-12. With the primary orientation toward the Lord explained, the consequences are described. To be acknowledged by God we must acknowledge His Son. It is not what you do that is most significant, but rather whom you trust. Trusting Christ means foregoing the world's approval. This trust is only manifest in a human soul through the work of the Holy Spirit in him. To deny the Spirit's work through unbelief is to blaspheme Him, and our denial of Christ is evidence of our blasphemy against the Spirit. The man who blasphemes against the Spirit should expect no forgiveness. At the same time, the Holy Spirit will be the One to guide and direct the believers in the extraordinary persecutions they will experience.

Family Discussion
Talk about the short-sightedness of a preoccupation with the things of this world at the expense of serving God in His kingdom.

Little Children: Talk about how the things of the world, like stuff and people's compliments, eventually pass away. Contrast the temporary nature of the things of this world with the enduring nature of what God promises.

Middle Children: Talk about seeking first the kingdom of God. Show how they can do that in their thinking (through reading and meditating on God's Word), in their speaking (stirring one another up toward love and good works), and in their actions (acting kindly and gently). Show how seeking the kingdom of God must flow out of a love for Christ.

Older Children: Look at verses 4-5 to discuss the fear of men as a powerful motivator. Talk about the importance of standing against the world through the power of the Holy Spirit at work in you. Talk about Christ's eternal perspective in this section by reviewing verse 5 together.

Family Singing
O Worship the King (Trinity Hymnal #2); My Portion Is the Lord (Psalter #119H)

Family Prayer
Ask the Lord to help you seek first His kingdom. Ask Him to make your family wise in His Word.

CHAPTER 34

Worrying About Stuff

TODAY'S READING: LUKE 12:13-34.

Introduction

Anxiety is a disbelief in God's ability to provide and is rooted in finding joy and comfort in material possessions instead. It constitutes a violation of the first commandment, showing a belief that the immediate is more significant than God. Instead we are to seek Him, who is the treasure of heavenly glory.

Bible Teaching

This passage addresses how Christians relate to the world in two ways. First, the parable of the rich fool teaches man to find contentment in what he has been given because his possessions are with him only for a short time. Second, by comparing people to birds, grass, and flowers, Jesus calls His disciples not to be anxious, but to trust God to supply all their needs.

◀ 12:13-21. God does not exist to give His followers what they want. However, the man who wanted Jesus to tell his brother to divide the inheritance with him (v. 13) was trying to use Jesus to get his stuff. But the things of this world can be taken away in the blink of an eye. Instead of focusing on worldly riches, the Christian needs to be rich with heavenly treasures. Covetousness, which Jesus is warning against, is a denial of the heavenly and focuses on our immediate possessions. A covetous spirit undermines the gospel in several ways:

First, covetousness tells *who* someone worships. Material possessions may be elevated to replace God. This sin is demonstrated in Scripture through Lot's wife (cf. Gen. 19:26). Her glance over her shoulder essentially said: 'I would rather be in my house in Sodom than following the Lord.' God was replaced in her life.

Second, covetousness shows the *level of trust* placed on God. In covetousness, gratitude is shallow, and trust is small. In covetousness, God's distribution of possessions is viewed as inadequate. The coveter is like Israel in the wilderness. They didn't trust that their current discomfort was temporary, and that God would fulfill His promise of bringing them into the Promised Land, so they grumbled against Him (cf. Exod. 16:2-3).

Finally, covetousness shows *disdain for God's great gift.* This man who is in the presence of Christ wants to use Him to get money. Instead of using money to worship the Savior he uses the Savior to worship money. The infinity of the gift of salvation is incomparably greater in value to anything on this earth. Man's primary concern should be over this treasure since he does not know when his life will be demanded of him.

◀ 12:22-34. In an argument from the lesser to the greater, Jesus also teaches that if God cares for the plants He will certainly give His beloved children what they need. This teaching deals with worry and anxiety. Verse 31 forms the hinge for this passage. Instead of being anxious for the things of this world, they are to seek first the kingdom of God, which is entered by faith. The things of this world will then grow strangely dim as we behold the wonderful splendor of heavenly treasure that will not spoil or fade.

Family Discussion

Lead your family in recognizing the glory of Christ far supersedes any other thing in the world. Show how proper faith in Christ removes the temptations for covetousness and worry or anxiety.

Little Children: Show your children how great a gift salvation is. Ask them what they think they would have to pay God to be forgiven and show that there is no amount. God is just, and cannot be bribed. Since the gift is so great, how should it compare to toys? Teach them contentment recognizes the greatness of God's gift for His people.

Middle Children: Show materialism as a sinful desire for the increase of possessions. Explain that covetousness is an expected secondary sin where we consider God's distributions to us to be inadequate. Talk about anxiety as a failure to believe God's ability or desire to honor His promise to provide for His people.

Older Children: J. C. Ryle says the following: 'Nothing is more common than an anxious and troubled spirit, and nothing so mars a believer's usefulness, and diminishes his inward peace.' Discuss.

Family Singing

O Worship the King (Trinity Hymnal #2); My Portion Is the Lord (Psalter #119H)

Family Prayer

Ask the Lord to forgive you for coveting and being anxious. Ask Him to grow you in your contentment in, and trust of, Him.

CHAPTER 35

Every-Day Christians

Introduction

In the parable of the soils Jesus gave the example of thorny soil, where the seed is choked out and never bears fruit. In today's verses, Jesus exhorts His disciples not to be like that soil. Their faith must be an 'every day' faith, not only serving God on certain occasions. Instead they must live in such a way to make their allegiance to God known. Christ has come as King to claim His people for Himself.

Bible Teaching

We can divide this passage up into Jesus' call for preparedness, exclusive loyalty to Christ, and recognition of His identity.

◀ 12:35-48. God's Spirit keeps and grows us in faith, yet, as Philippians 2:12-13 shows us, there is also an element of human responsibility in this process. God gives His children the strength, and they work out their salvation in fear and trembling. Part of this work is to always be prepared for Christ's return. He shows that, though God may seem far removed, our faith in Him means we believe Him when He says His judgment against sin will come in an instant. When it does, many will prove themselves to be plants choked out by the worries and lusts of this world. In contrast, those preserved in their faith will have great blessing (v. 43). Blessing is the nearness and presence of God (cf. Ps. 21:6). Its opposite, cursing, is when God's presence is removed (cf. Gen. 4:12). In its final manifestation, blessing brings a man before God in heaven while cursing separates him from God in hell.

◀ 12:49-53. The seed planted among the thorns is a picture of a person who has trouble committing himself fully to Lord. Yet Jesus could not draw the lines more clearly. Jesus has not come to make everyone get along but to show there are only two kinds of people: Christians and non-Christians. These two categories transcend all other relational bonds. Christians are not ruled by their family ties but by their heavenly King. They are to seek first

His kingdom, trusting Him to provide. They do not depend partially on man and partially on God, but cast themselves completely on the Lord.

◀ 12:54-59. Jesus has come and His identity cannot be missed. Those who count themselves wise in the interpretation of natural signs do not recognize the prophecies fulfilled in Christ. Those who think themselves clever in the ways of the world completely misjudge Jesus of Nazareth. If they persist in this judgment they will never escape their eternal debt.

Family Discussion

Consider how easy it is to turn aside from Christ in the middle of temptation. Yet above all we are to long for His blessing and shudder at His cursing.

Little Children: Talk about who gives faith. Look at Ephesians 2:8-10 for help. Talk about what is required once faith is given. Ask them if they can be a believer and an unbeliever at the same time. What should a believer do with God's commandments?

Middle Children: Show the difference between blessing and cursing from Psalm 21:6 and Genesis 4:12. How does heaven manifest blessing in the most perfect way? How does hell manifest God's curse?

Older Children: In verses 49-53 Jesus talks about bringing division. Talk about faith in Him as the dividing line. Discuss the dangers of peer pressure. Talk about discerning between those who would encourage you to live in blessing (i.e. the presence of God) as opposed to those who would lead you away from Him.

Family Singing

O for a Thousand Tongues to Sing (Trinity Hymnal #164); O Lord, Our Lord (Psalter #8A)

Family Prayer

Pray that God would help you persevere in faith. Ask Him for growth in your spiritual walk.

CHAPTER 36

About Repentance

Introduction

These verses teach the urgency of repentance of sin before the God who secured our redemption and His patience with us. Repentance is worked in any Christian by the Holy Spirit. The *Westminster Confession of Faith* describes repentance as so significant that 'none may expect pardon without it.'[1] Today's verses teach the crucial role repentance plays in the Christian life.

Bible Teaching

These verses can be divided into Jesus' teaching about the need for repentance, God's great patience in granting time to repent, and the call to repentance by His Word.

◀ 13:1-5. When the *Westminster Confession of Faith* calls repentance a necessity for pardon, it appeals to these verses in Luke for its justification. The question asked of Jesus about the Galileans, who had their blood mingled with their sacrifices, is a question that assumes works-righteousness. The question assumes God renders judgment based on man's performance. Jesus, ignoring the faults in this question and the corresponding inquiry about the tower of Siloam, addresses what is truly necessary to avoid God's judgment: repentance (vv. 3, 5). Repentance, not to be confused with regret, involves several things. Regret simply laments the effects of getting caught in sin. Repentance is far deeper. First, repentance acknowledges sin and how grievous it is before the Lord. Second, it recognizes God's mercy in forgiving sinners. Third, it seeks this forgiveness in Christ alone. Finally, it turns from sin to God, seeking to live obediently by Christ's power at work in him. No one can be a citizen of the kingdom of God and continue living like a citizen of the kingdom of darkness.

◀ 13:6-9. Repentance is like a tree bearing fruit. Christians can be slow to repent despite the warning of God's Word. In His illustration of the vinedresser,

---

1. *Westminster Confession of Faith*, Chapter 15.3.

Jesus shows God's patience toward those whose fruit is stunted. Although He would be justified in pruning the unfruitful branches and throwing them into the fire, He nurtures His weak branches to make them fruitful. However, the dire warning is that there will come a day when those who will not repent will be destroyed.

◀ 13:10-17. God's grace to His creation is further stressed in the healing of a woman on the Sabbath. Though she had suffered eighteen years with this disability, the synagogue ruler became indignant at her healing. Jesus' response shows God's kindness even in the treatment of beasts of burden. However, the traditions of the Pharisees had hidden and distorted the graciousness of God for the Sabbath. This day was meant to be a day of worship and rest in the God of grace. It had become a day of looking over your shoulder to see if man's tradition had been satisfied.

Family Discussion
Talk about the importance of repentance of sin to God in the life of the believer.

Little Children: Discuss how someone's actions show whether they are truly repentant. Talk about repentance as turning around on your path because you know it is not a path that honors God.

Middle Children: Talk about the difference between regret and repentance. Show how you might regret getting caught without thinking of the wickedness of your sin and the need for forgiveness from Christ. Show them regret is not repentance.

Older Children: Talk about the *Westminster Confession of Faith* quote that none can expect pardon without repentance. What does that mean for Christians who do not turn from their sin? Talk about the four aspects of repentance.

Family Singing
O the Deep, Deep Love of Jesus (Trinity Hymnal #535); That Man Is Blessed (Psalter #1A)

Family Prayer
Ask the Lord to forgive your sins and to give you grace and mercy as you seek to live according to His Word.

CHAPTER 37

The Narrow Gate Only

TODAY'S READING: LUKE 13:18-35.

Introduction

This passage discusses the kingdom of God again. There is but a narrow door through which to enter God's presence. Many will fail to enter through that door. Even the people of Jerusalem, God's covenant people, will balk at the One who would be their Door.

Bible Teaching

We can easily see the progression of Jesus' teaching by breaking this passage down into the following three parts:

◀ 13:18-21. The implication of the parables of the mustard seed and leaven is that, though the kingdom of God begins small and insignificant, there will be pervasive growth. Rather than speaking of its numerical size, these parables deal with the power or influence of the kingdom of God. Though the disciples of Jesus may seem insignificant, the Holy Spirit will use these men as His witnesses in 'Jerusalem and in all Judea and Samaria, and to the end of the earth' (Acts 1:8) to speak of Christ and His work of redemption.

◀ 13:22-30. When one who heard Jesus' teaching asked Him if only few will be chosen, He answers by describing a door. Many will seek to enter through it, but will be rejected. Jesus is not teaching here that people want to enter into His presence but are refused. Rather, there are many who seek to find a way to enter the presence of God while ignoring the Door He has appointed for this purpose: Christ. When they seek God's acceptance (v. 25b) God will not recognize them because Christ is our only Mediator. Jesus warns of the impending judgment for those who reject Christ. They will be cast out into a place of weeping and gnashing of teeth. They will weep, while Abraham and his children of the faith from all over the world (v. 29) are accepted into God's presence.

◀ 13:31-35. After reported threats from Herod, Jesus continues His movement toward Jerusalem. Since Peter's confession He moves steadily toward Israel's capital. He goes to Jerusalem knowing death awaits Him. The citizens there have a long history of turning away from the prophets. Since the kingdom's influence is strong but few will enter into her, this section describes those foolish enough to turn away. Some of them will be the people of Jerusalem who have enjoyed centuries of covenant privilege. The sin of Jerusalem grieves the Savior. Indeed, He is grieved by all sin and rebellion.

Family Discussion

Discuss the idea of the people of God as a remnant and that God's power is not realized in this age but in the age to come.

Little Children: Talk to your children about the persecuted church. How is the power of the kingdom seen in the persecuted church? Talk about how God gives the church power and strength even if she is relatively small and weak.

Middle Children: From verse 27 talk about the consequence of trying to enter apart from the narrow door. Look at John 10:7-9 and refute the idea there are many ways to God. Discuss Christ as the only entrance, and encourage your children to ask the Lord to bring them in by the narrow gate.

Older Children: Talk about the influence of the kingdom of God despite its small size. Think of examples in Scripture where the influence of God's kingdom was felt despite its size: Daniel and his friends, Elijah versus Baal's priests, the early New Testament church, and other examples. Talk about God's power at work in these circumstances.

Family Singing

The Church's One Foundation (Trinity Hymnal #347); God Is Our Refuge and Our Strength (Psalter #46B)

Family Prayer

Ask God to strengthen your reliance on Christ alone for salvation. Thank God for His mercy in calling all nations to Himself.

CHAPTER 38

For Mercy's Sake

TODAY'S READING: LUKE 14:1-6.

Introduction

Previously, Jesus addressed the Pharisees' Sabbath traditions (cf. Luke 6:1-5 – chapter 14). Here He continues to teach the biblical principle of the Sabbath including God's clear intent in this commmandment. Jesus shows the spirit of what it means to honor the Sabbath. Built into this day of rest is the understanding of the appropriateness of works of mercy.

Bible Teaching

Since our passage is small, we can break up the paragraph to clearly see the development of Jesus' teaching on the Sabbath:

◀ 14:1-2. Here we are reintroduced to the Pharisees. These men, who loved their traditions more than anything, had grown increasingly suspicious of Jesus. They had not yet completely given in to their hatred. However, as He is with them at dinner, they are keeping a close eye on Him, seeing if He would yet again defy their traditions. The tension is based around a man with dropsy, a disease where the body retains fluids in the cavities and tissues of the body. It is possible the Pharisees introduced this man to the scene for the purpose of catching Jesus or that, by God's providence, the man came to the dinner party.

◀ 14:3-4a. Jesus senses the test of the Pharisees and addresses the issue head-on. He asks them whether the law prohibits healing on the Sabbath. The Pharisees remain silent. They employ the 'silent treatment' sometime later when they ask Jesus by whose authority He preaches and teaches (cf. Luke 20:3-7). Discerning the disingenuousness of their question, Jesus asks them whether John the Baptist's baptism is from heaven or from man. Seeing that either answer opens them up to criticism, they prefer to remain silent. They use the same tactic in response to Jesus' question here as well. Their concern is not truth, but the preservation of right appearances.

◀ 14:4b-6. In response, Jesus heals the man on the spot. He shows they would be merciful to an animal acting on their behalf on the Sabbath. How much more should they do so in the case of men? God's mercy should be displayed liberally, especially on the Sabbath day, a day in which God's people have the special privilege of worshiping the Lord. This passage is not making provision for those who could not bother to rightly order their affairs so they could enjoy a Sabbath rest. Rather, Jesus is teaching that to perform a work of mercy or necessity is entirely within keeping of the fourth commandment.

Family Discussion

Take some time to examine your own attitudes toward the Sabbath.

Little Children: Talk about what a work of mercy is. Ask them if it is ever disobedient to God to help someone who is sick. Try to think of different ways your family can show God's mercy to others in keeping with the fourth commandment.

Middle Children: How can we see the Pharisees are not interested in the truth (cf. also Luke 20:3-7)? Can they then be interested in Christ (cf. John 14:6)? What are some ways you are tempted to put up a good front when, in fact, your hearts have wandered far from the Lord?

Older Children: Talk about preparing yourself for the Sabbath and an anticipation of our heavenly rest. What is the difference between your ox being in a ditch and doing homework on the Lord's Day? Should we delight in the rest and worship of the Sabbath?

Family Singing

How Firm a Foundation (Trinity Hymnal #94); My Portion Is the Lord (Psalter #119H)

Family Prayer

Ask the Lord to help you honor Him in your Sabbath-keeping. Ask Him to protect you against vain external compliance.

CHAPTER 39

The Glory of Humility

TODAY'S READING: LUKE 14:7-24.

Introduction

Jesus is still at the Pharisee's house when He observes something about the practice of the people: they all are preoccupied with self-promotion. Jesus uses this opportunity to teach on humility, perfectly modeled for us in Christ.

Bible Teaching

Jesus gives two lessons on humility in this passage:

◀ 14:7-11. First Jesus uses a story to illustrate that when man seeks his own glory, his shame will be greater when his ambitions are denied. Jesus observed the people at the Pharisee's house trying to express their own significance. Their preoccupation should be with the Lord's glory. Glory for His Father is what Christ seeks to establish in His earthly ministry (cf. John 13:31). Jesus is not encouraging the manipulation of appearances in verse 10. Instead, He urges the people toward true humility. He teaches the lesson found in Philippians 2:3-4 which instructs us to consider other people's needs first by way of imitation of Christ. If in humility you consider yourself least and are elevated to a position of honor, you will truly be honored. You will be honored because you have honored the Lord.

◀ 14:12-24. Jesus' second parable deals with a hypothetical banquet. The banquet Jesus is attending seems to be organized solely to establish connections. It is an exercise in self-promotion. But the Christian life is not about self-promotion, but serving Christ. Instead of hosting for their own benefit, He encourages them to think first of the interests of others. This kind of service is heavenly service (v. 14). Lest they are led astray by merely external obedience, Jesus brings them back to their motivation for their own service: the gospel. God has brought unworthy sinners to His banquet (v. 21) through the blood of Christ. He will suffer and die so His people can be free from sin's guilt. These worthless ones, the very people of God, replace those who seem to be worthwhile but make excuses. Their excuses deal with their own interests. In response, Jesus delivers an ominous warning in the last verse of the passage: '...none of those men who were invited shall taste my banquet.' The general call of God's Word goes out, and man must humble himself before it, clinging to Christ alone for mercy. If he dismisses the call of the gospel, he will be withheld from the banquet of the King.

Family Discussion

True humility is rarely seen because it is expressed only through the Spirit at work in the redeemed. Those who are touted as humble men in the culture do not usually practice true biblical humility. Men like Mahatma Gandhi, though humble in appearance, are actually idolaters who defy the only Living and True God. Talk together about true biblical humility.

Little Children: Discuss what it means to be humble. Read Philippians 2:3-4 together. Ask them for examples of how people can be humble. Talk to them about the humility of Christ in coming to earth. Show them how Christ's humility is the foundation for our humility.

Middle Children: Talk about the behavior of the Pharisees. Talk about how they elevated man over God in their love for tradition (see Luke 6:1-5). How does Jesus teach them to consider others before themselves in the two parables?

Older Children: Discuss how Jesus is not encouraging manipulation in v. 10. Discuss how understanding man's sinful nature helps with humility. How does their sin make them gracious with their fellow man?

Family Singing

A Mighty Fortress Is Our God (Trinity Hymnal #92); Your Word's a Lamp (Psalter #119N)

Family Prayer

Ask the Lord to help you grow in your understanding of your sin. Pray that you would be able to see the glory of God and be humbled.

CHAPTER 40

Cost Analysis

TODAY'S READING: LUKE 14:25-35.

Introduction

Today's topic is suffering for Christ's sake. The willingness to suffer for Christ is a necessary component of Christian life and reflects our assessment of Jesus' gift of salvation. An unwillingness to suffer for Christ shows we think the comforts of this life are more valuable than He is.

Bible Teaching

Today's reading deals with the cost of discipleship and includes a short addendum that reinforces the main point.

◀ 14:25-33. Large crowds come to hear Jesus' teaching and see His miracles, even following Him on His journeys. But Jesus begins teaching less palatable things and making exclusive statements. On three different occasions, Jesus sets forth a condition, which if not met, disqualifies people from being His disciples (vv. 26, 27, 33).

The first statement shows His disciples must value their relationship with Christ above all others (v. 26). Of course, our love for Christ is based on His initial love for man (cf. 1 John 4:19). His sacrifice for His people should make them value Him over anything and anyone else. Even the most intimate relationships must be despised in favor of Christ: parents, spouses, children, and siblings. Jesus does not mean that unless His disciples hate their parents, siblings, children, or spouses they cannot be His disciple, but their love for Jesus must be primary.

The second statement shows Christ's disciples must be willing to suffer (v. 27). The expression 'to bear your cross' means to carry on in the face of hardship. All believers should question their willingness to suffer for Christ, but it is rarely done in Western culture. The true disciple will bear up under a season of suffering, counting the cost of knowing Christ as worthwhile. This point is illustrated by Christ through the image of the king and his army.

The final statement teaches the disciples should value their relationship with Christ over worldly possessions (v. 33). For our brothers in persecuted lands, this challenge is often a present reality. Even in Western nations God has asked people to give up successful businesses to be faithful to Christ. Their choices in these difficult circumstances show their allegiances. Their choices indicate the value they place on Christ.

◀ 14:34-35. In this final synopsis Jesus indicates the severity of being a lukewarm disciple. The disciples live to glorify God in their thoughts, words, and actions. If this motivation is not found in them, they are good for nothing except to be thrown away. Their decisions reveal the condition of their hearts. If the Spirit lives in them, they will prefer Christ over any relationship, the comforts of this life, and all their possessions.

Family Discussion
Talk about the importance of being willing to deny all because Christ is more valuable to them than anything else.

Little Children: Talk about why they should love God more than anything else. Talk about how they love people by giving them a hug or a present. Talk about how they love God by following Him.

Middle Children: Talk about each of the three challenges Jesus issues in verses 25-33. When might they be forced to choose between loved ones, or possessions, and Christ? Ask them if they are willing to suffer for Christ. Why?

Older Children: Talk about Jesus' challenge to count the cost of what it means to follow Him. Discuss what things are valued in the culture and whether they are willing to abandon them all for the sake of following Christ. Is Christ less significant than anything?

Family Singing
Come Thou Long Expected Jesus (Trinity Hymnal #196); Bless the Lord, My Soul (Psalter #103B)

Family Prayer
Pray for the courage of the persecuted church and ask God to make you willing to abandon all in service of Christ.

CHAPTER 41

Lost and Found

TODAY'S READING: LUKE 15:1-32.

Introduction

The three parables recorded in today's passage address the return of a backslider. The first two tell of the joy in heaven that accompanies such a return. But the third parable adds what change takes place in the heart of the repentant sinner and speaks of our right response.

Bible Teaching

All three parables come in response to the Pharisees who disapproved of the presence of 'sinners' with Jesus. They miss that Jesus came to die on the Cross for people such as these.

◀ 15:1-7. The first parable pictures a shepherd who loses one of his sheep. The one lost sheep represents the straying brother or sister. Notice the sheep do not look for the shepherd, but he for them. The point Jesus draws is clear: God seeks after sinners and, when they are reclaimed, there is more joy in heaven than over the others who need not repent, in the sense of their initial turning unto Christ.

◀ 15:8-10. The next parable uses coins to teach the same thing. When a precious coin goes missing the owner will look for it diligently. When the owner finds the coin again, she rejoices over having found it, much like someone might when they find lost keys or a missing cell phone. Jesus emphasizes the joy experienced in heaven over true repentance.

◀ 15:11-32. The last parable represents the spiritual condition of the backslider. The Prodigal Son leaves his father's home. He lives a debauched life and seems to have forgotten his father. So it is with the backsliding Christian. He may appear to have turned his back on Christ and the gospel. However, he is in the grip of his Savior, and there will come a point when he will realize his desperate condition and long to be with his Father again. The prodigal manifests grief over his sin and returns to his father's house seeking only his forgiveness. In addition to teaching about the backslider, the parable also challenges sinful attitudes, such as the Pharisees are manifesting (v. 2), toward the one who is repenting by its description of the older brother (vv. 25-30). The elder brother resents the father's kindness to the prodigal. Likewise, the Pharisees may do what is right on the outside, but they lack the joy that belongs to the angels and the Father at the return of a backslider. Jesus, through these parables, convicts the Pharisees for this lack of joy. He invites them to share in the joys of heaven where the cost of purchasing these lost people is known: the blood of Christ.

Family Discussion

Discuss how self-righteous pride puts man at odds with heavenly joy.

Little Children: Talk about the joy of heaven in the three parables. Ask if they would be happy if they lost their favorite toy and then found it again. Talk about how the angels and God Himself rejoice in that way when people repent of their sin.

Middle Children: Show the similarity between the Pharisees and the older brother. Talk about how understanding man's nature and the consequence of sin should make them delight in a fellow-sinner's repentance. Talk about pride as the root that prevents the Pharisees from embracing 'sinners.'

Older Children: Talk about their self-righteous hearts. Discuss how people end up thinking like the Pharisees. Show how a proper understanding of their sin protects them against pride. How would this teaching affect their interaction with new members of your church?

Family Singing

Joy to the World, the Lord Is Come (Trinity Hymnal #195); All Like Mount Zion Unmoved Shall Endure (Psalter #125)

Family Prayer

Ask the Lord to guard you against pride and to help you to see your own sin.

CHAPTER 42

The Christian and Money

TODAY'S READING: LUKE 16:1-18.

Introduction

Wealth itself is not sinful, but many attitudes that accompany it are. Culturally it is more common for wealth to be used to serve 'self.' Jesus, in this passage, teaches wealth is not to be held on to but rather administered to God's glory.

Bible Teaching

In the treatment of this subject, we can divide our passage into the parable, its meaning, its response, and then an example.

◀ 16:1-9. Jesus is not advocating using money to buy friends (v. 9). Instead He urges the disciples to please those who would welcome them into 'the eternal dwellings' both in their use of and attitude toward money. That means wealth is to be used to please God. As the manager cut the bills owed to his master to please the debtors, so we are to be willing to use wealth to honor God, managing it as stewards of His possessions.

◀ 16:10-13. Jesus expands His teaching on finances to deal with faithfulness. Jesus equates faithfulness in wealth as a test. In the management of riches, a person's qualifications for the heavenly blessings are proved or denied. The treatment of wealth shows which master a man serves: God or money. Either he expends himself in God's service, or he does so in the pursuit of money (cf. Matt. 6:24).

◀ 16:14-17. Jesus' discourse convicts the Pharisees because they loved money. Jesus further inflames their anger against Him by pointing out their self-righteousness, which is an abomination before the Lord (v. 15). Verse 16 seems to imply that anyone can force his way into the kingdom of God. However, the kingdom of God is entered only by being born again (cf. John 3:3, 5). Instead this verse points to the forceful pursuit of God's kingdom by faith for those enabled to do so by the Holy Spirit. The Pharisees' action is so grievous because they fail to follow the Law which, in summary form, teaches us to love God with all our hearts (cf. Deut. 6:4). Instead they choose to love self. But through the good news of the kingdom, man is called to repentance and love for God as a result of his forgiveness purchased by Christ.

◀ 16:18. Love of self is manifest in our sin. Love for money or our neglect of marriage vows are attempts to make God's Law void, which is not possible (v. 17). Divorce for unbiblical grounds does not free you from your marriage covenant. Therefore, to remarry after unlawful divorce makes you an adulterer. The church of Christ should heed these words, especially in our day where unlawful divorce is rampant.

Family Discussion
Discuss idolatry in the unhealthy attitudes we may have toward money.

Little Children: Talk about God's provision for them. Teach that God gives them everything and that they should thank Him. Explain the reason for thanking God before eating. Talk about God's grace to them and how they should love Him for it.

Middle Children: Talk about how riches can be used well or poorly. Show how an unhealthy pursuit of wealth is idolatrous. Talk about idolatry as anything that is counted as more important or lovely than God. Look especially at verses 10-11.

Older Children: Show how the manager used wealth to gain the favor of others. Talk about how the Christian is not seeking to please man but One who will welcome them into eternal dwellings (v. 9). What about tithing? Is it wrong to be wealthy?

Family Singing
King of Nations, Hear Our Prayer (Trinity Hymnal #713); O All You Nations of the Earth (Psalter #117A)

Family Prayer
Ask the Lord to protect you from materialism and help you use His possessions wisely as a steward in His kingdom.

CHAPTER 43

Heaven and Hell

TODAY'S READING: LUKE 16:19-31.

Introduction

In today's parable, Jesus teaches the urgency of coming to faith in Him while we are alive. Once we die, any chance for reconciliation is gone. But more than just a stark warning, Jesus shows how this way of redemption can be known.

Bible Teaching

This parable can be divided into two sections. The first deals with the finality of death. The second deals with the method God uses to inform the world of the nature of salvation and the need for repentance.

◀ 16:19-26. Man's eternal condition is divided into two options: those who suffer in hell and those who enjoy the blessings of heaven. The rich man in hell cries out in agony, looking for relief from his suffering. Please note, the parable is not meant to describe the geographical proximity of heaven and hell or whether we will have conversations with those on the other side of the chasm. Instead, the parable is meant to show that once death comes, there is no way to change your eternal dwelling. You will either be in heaven or hell. This lesson shows the urgency of repentance and turning from sin to God. Some scoff at this urgency because they recognize mortality in all except themselves. Despite the folly of man, Jesus calls them to repent now while it is still possible.

◀ 16:27-31. As the parable develops, the words of the rich man shift from his own condition to that of his living relatives. The rich man recognizes they are facing the same fate as he is and seeks to spare them. He asks Abraham to send Lazarus as a supernatural warning. However, the miracles alone are never enough to persuade a sinner to come to God in repentance. For example, the Gerasenes ask Jesus to depart in response to His miracle (cf. Luke 8:37). The parable points away from the miracles and toward His Word. The brothers have all the warning they need because they have Moses and the prophets. These are sufficient to warn anyone of his need for a Savior (cf. Gen. 3:15) and display the promise that He is coming to bear our guilt (cf. Isa. 53 or Lev. 16:20-22). The miracles confirm the Word of God, but they are secondary, not primary. God's Word is primary.

Family Discussion

Talk about the importance of faith in Christ and His Word to teach all that is needed to know about faith and practice.

Little Children: Talk about the importance of seeking heaven's glory while we have the chance. Show how Christ secures this glory for them when they turn to Him in repentance. Talk about how God's Word shows them what it means to repent of sin.

Middle Children: Talk about how there are only two eternal destinations: heaven or hell. Talk about the finality of those destinations after death. Discuss how God's Word is enough to teach them what they are to believe about God and how they are to live for Him.

Older Children: Talk about the need for people to trust the Word of God. Since the Word of God is central in rescuing a person from hell, show how it is not loving to withhold the Word from someone out of fear of offending him. How can families and churches fail to bring the life-giving message to the world? What might be the disastrous result of this neglect?

Family Singing

Christ, Whose Glory Fills the Sky (Trinity Hymnal #398); Why Do Gentile Nations Rage (Psalter #2B)

Family Prayer

Ask the Lord to help you understand the truth of His Word. Ask Him to use you to be a messenger of hope to a fallen world.

CHAPTER 44

Faith and Works

TODAY'S READING: LUKE 17:1-19.

Introduction

The three sections of today's text may seem unrelated at first, but they are tied together through the common theme of the relationship between faith and works. Actions express faith commitments. Works are simply an expression of the embrace or denial of Christ's work on the Cross.

Bible Teaching

These verses move between expressions of works and faith. Understanding both is crucial to see that righteousness is not the result of works. It is only when obedience flows from faith in God that it is a true expression of love for God.

◀ 17:1-6. Temptation is not an individual problem. Certainly attention must be paid to private sins (v. 3), but sin is also the Christian community's problem. Therefore, within the church there is a responsibility to identify instances of sin in others' lives. The motivation of this confrontation is to keep them from being like those who are cast into the sea with a millstone around their neck (v. 2). Sometimes reproofs are perceived as unwelcome intrusions. Certainly, an ungracious address of someone's sin can lead to discouragement. However, when the Christian comes in humility (cf. Gal. 6:1), his words actually protect and encourage. The goal of correction is the repentance of the sinner and, if and when he repents, forgiveness must immediately be offered. The disciples recognize they need faith to accomplish this command (v. 5), which Christ confirms.

◀ 17:7-10. Anticipating man's confidence in his 'good deeds,' Jesus teaches works give us no merit. When works are carried out perfectly, which they never are, they are at best only what God requires. When a servant does his work, he is not praised because his service is expected. So it is with man's obedience. God made man and he is therefore obligated to his Creator. He should do what God commands.

◀ 17:11-19. That is not to say works are insignificant. Works are evidence of salvation purchased by the blood of Christ. In the cleansing of the ten lepers,

Jesus makes this point abundantly clear. All of the lepers cry out to Jesus for mercy and He sends them on their way to the priests. As they realize they are healed, only one, a Samaritan, returns to thank Jesus for what He has done for him. Christ's work in him leads him to worship (v. 16). Works, done in response to redemption accomplished in Christ, are recognized as an evidence of faith.

Family Discussion

Discuss moralistic works as deeds done as an end in themselves versus evangelical works which express love for what Christ has accomplished for the sinner.

Little Children: Ask your children if it is important to obey God. Why? Talk about the importance of loving God for saving them from their sins. Show how obeying God is a way of showing Him they love Him (cf. 1 John 5:3).

Middle Children: Talk about the Samaritan leper. How is his action different from the other nine lepers? How do the nine fail to give praise to God? How does the Samaritan's action demonstrate faith (v. 19)? Talk about the importance of showing our faith in action.

Older Children: Talk about their responsibility toward each other when it comes to sin. Look at Galatians 6:1-2 and discuss their attitude in confronting sin. Talk about the importance of forgiveness. Read Colossians 3:13 for the right attitude in forgiveness.

Family Singing

Come Thou Long Expected Jesus (Trinity Hymnal #196); O All You Nations of the Earth (Psalter #117A)

Family Prayer

Pray for the growth of your faith that you would rightly live for God. Ask Him to make your heart tender toward sin.

CHAPTER 45

When Christ Returns

Introduction

In today's verses Luke records Jesus' teaching on His return. Jesus inaugurates His kingdom at His birth and consummates it at His second coming. So His people can rest in the present kingdom and live in the hope of its future, final completion.

Bible Teaching

The Pharisees ask a question of the coming of the kingdom of God. Jesus answers it in three parts: first, He addresses the Pharisees, second, His disciples, and third, the implications for those outside the kingdom.

◀ 17:20-21. The nature of the Pharisees' question can be inferred from Jesus' response. The Pharisees want to be able to identify the coming kingdom. What they mean by 'the kingdom' is the Davidic monarchy. However, Jesus corrects their misconceptions, noting that the kingdom of God is in their midst even as they speak. Christ, our King, has come to establish His spiritual kingdom made up of the family of faith.

◀ 17:22-35. These verses overlap a little with the Olivet Discourse (Matt. 24–25). In His address to His disciples Jesus expands on His answer to the Pharisees. Jesus knows their desire to predict His return will only be heightened when He ascends into heaven. Jesus warns His disciples to ignore the cries of those who would point to His return. It will be evident to all when it happens, but trying to predict its arrival is futile. To make His point, Jesus illustrates from the days of Noah. Life was going on as usual for Noah and Lot's neighbors in Sodom and Gomorrah, yet suddenly judgment was upon them and they were not prepared. The difference between Lot and Sodom is found in how they relate to God. It is only by faith in Him that we enter the kingdom of God. This distinction is not based on outward appearance. Two people doing the same things will be divided based on the presence or absence of faith.

◀ 17:37. The curiosity of the disciples does not revolve around questions of timing or inclusion. Rather they want to know where these people will be taken. Jesus does not deal with geography, but says that wherever the spiritually dead may find themselves, the judgment will come upon them and feed on their carcasses. There is no escaping it.

Family Discussion

Discuss the importance of complete surrender to Christ. Also discuss how this surrender will be manifested at all times, not only when we expect His coming.

Little Children: Talk about what it is like to live in a kingdom. How should the king's subjects behave? Do they only have to obey the king if they think he is watching them? Talk about the importance of loving God all the time. How does Lot's wife betray her love of God?

Middle Children: Talk about the spiritual nature of the kingdom of God. How is the kingdom of God different than the national identities of countries? Talk about God's gift of faith to Noah compared to his contemporaries. Show how Lot believed God's messengers while the people of Sodom and Gomorrah rejected them.

Older Children: Talk about the danger in trying to predict the second coming of Christ. Show how verse 30 makes it clear that Jesus will come at an unexpected time. Talk about how knowing that He will come is far more significant than when He will come. How does verse 33 guide our lives as we wait for Christ's return?

Family Singing

O Worship the King (Trinity Hymnal #2); O Lord, Our Lord (Psalter #8A)

Family Prayer

Pray that the Lord would keep you until He returns. Ask Him to return quickly.

CHAPTER 46

God Grants Mercy

TODAY'S READING: LUKE 18:1-17.

Introduction

The common thread of these verses is found in the understanding of man's relationship with God. Prayers to God and attitudes about other people are shaped by the understanding of who man is in his natural relation to God.

Bible Teaching

Our passage can be divided along the lines of the three separate lessons:

◀ 18:1-8. The explanation for these parables is conveniently stated up front. The first parable is given by Jesus to teach persistence in prayer. Persistence does not mean every request made of God will be granted. However, justice will be granted to God's people no matter how long they must wait (v. 8). Jesus teaches from the lesser to the greater. If the godless judge will grant justice, how much more will the righteous Heavenly Father? So if specific requests are not granted (cf. 2 Cor. 12:7-9), appeals to God for justice can be confidently known to be granted in His most wise timing.

◀ 18:9-14. Justice comes to man as a result of God's gracious gift. Of course, in his pride he wants to take credit for his standing, but Jesus shows such desires and attempts are vanity. He does so through the parable of the Pharisee and tax collector. The former was confident in his own works as demonstrated by his prayer (vv. 11-12). He comes to God thinking his fasting and tithing establish his superiority over others. The tax collector is not confident in himself at all. Instead he comes to the Lord in humility, seeking God's mercy because he knows himself to be a sinner. The one who thinks himself superior is actually inferior.

◀ 18:15-17. In the very next verses, the disciples disregard Jesus and imitate the Pharisee of the parable. They think children are too insignificant to take up Jesus' time. The disciples seem to think their questions and needs are far more significant than those of little children. But Christ affirms both the attitude and significance of children; they belong to the kingdom of God.

Children are completely dependent on the provision of their parents. This dependence is even more significant when it comes to parents introducing or, in a sense, bringing their children to Christ. Family worship, prayer, church attendance, and godly example are all different ways in which we bring our children to Christ. And for all people, if they do not come completely dependent on the mercy of God found through Christ, they behave as the the Pharisee from verses 9-14.

Family Discussion

Approach this discussion with your family in great humility, impressing your imperfections and inability to contribute to your salvation.

Little Children: Talk about sin and how they all commit sins. Tell them the importance of taking these sins to Christ, knowing He will welcome them if they come by faith. Show them how Jesus wants them to come (v. 16). Talk about His great love for His children.

Middle Children: Talk about the words of the Pharisee versus the tax collector. Show the pride of the Pharisee. Talk about how the tax collector's posture shows humility. Talk about different ways they might demonstrate a spirit of self-righteousness or humility.

Older Children: Talk about Jesus' argument from lesser to greater in the parable of the unjust judge (vv. 1-8). Show how this parable is not teaching that they will always get what they want if they ask often enough. Look at James 4:3 and Luke 22:42 for examples of unanswered prayer and different reasons for them.

Family Singing

O the Deep, Deep Love of Jesus (Trinity Hymnal #535); Bless the Lord, My Soul (Psalter #103B)

Family Prayer

Ask the Lord to bless you with humility. Pray that He would convict you of pride wherever it may be found.

CHAPTER 47

Prophecy and Worship

TODAY'S READING: LUKE 18:18-43.

Introduction

In these verses we see the necessity of the denial of this world by Christ's disciples. The young ruler clung to his wealth, but the Son of Man does not even cling to His own life. He surrenders all in service of the Father and expects the same of His disciples.

Bible Teaching

In dividing up this passage among the three different accounts, we will be able to follow a connecting thread throughout:

◀ 18:18-30. In this account, the young ruler is seeking to justify himself. He wants to know what action he has to take (v. 18) to inherit eternal life. Jesus points the man to the Law of God in order to show his inability to obey it. However, this man persists in his self-righteousness, claiming he had obeyed God's Law from his childhood. Jesus, without addressing the folly of his previous statement, simply pinpoints this man's overarching sin: idolatry. The rich young ruler realizes he is not willing to surrender his wealth, and he leaves. Jesus teaches His disciples that only God can change an idolatrous heart (v. 27). Whatever God may ask His people to surrender, they should be willing to leave it all behind on the altar of their hearts.

◀ 18:31-34. As if to paint a contrasting picture, the next account speaks of the humiliation of the Son of Man in His service of the Father. He will be mocked, flogged, and killed, but on the third day He will rise again. Though the disciples did not understand this lesson at the time, Luke's purpose in recording it is for those who come after as they read of Christ's fulfillment of these predictions. Whereas the rich young ruler wanted only to serve for his own advancement, Jesus surrenders all to do His Father's bidding.

◀ 18:35-43. The healing of the beggar reinforces the proper response of those who are spared by God. What the young ruler despised, the healed beggar rejoices over. This blind man saw more clearly than many of his day. He recognized Jesus as the promised Messiah and asked for His mercy. His boldness in asking showed his faith, and Jesus provides healing. This man responds by following Jesus. Nothing could make him leave his Savior's side. He worships him and glorifies God. His worship causes the worship of God by the people who had witnessed the healing too.

Family Discussion

Talk about turning away from idols when joined to Christ, and what it means to respond with worship over His eternal gift of salvation.

Little Children: Ask your children what the young ruler loved more: Jesus or his money. Show them how, when he walked away from Jesus, he was showing the greater love he had for his riches. Talk about man's main goal being to glorify God and enjoy Him and the great reward of heaven that comes by faith.

Middle Children: In contrast to the limits of what the young ruler is willing to do to serve God, what is Jesus willing to do (vv. 31-34)? Talk to your children about how they benefit from Christ's death. How do they learn from the healed blind beggar's response in verse 43?

Older Children: The rich young ruler asked what he could *do* to inherit eternal life. Talk about their inability to do anything to inherit life by considering the Total Depravity of man. How is his self-assessment in verse 21 flawed? How are they tempted to do the same?

Family Singing

A Mighty Fortress Is Our God (Trinity Hymnal #92); Who With God Most High Finds Shelter (Psalter #91A)

Family Prayer

Ask the Lord to protect you against self-righteousness. Ask Him to help you delight in His gracious gifts to you.

CHAPTER 48

Bearing Fruit Is Not an Option

TODAY'S READING: LUKE 19:1-27.

Introduction

The parables in today's passage are familiar. First, Christ welcomes Zacchaeus into the kingdom of God as a friend based on what he believes. He is no longer viewed as an enemy because he recognizes Christ's reign over him. Second, in the parable of the minas, Christ's enemies are shown to be those who grumble against Him. These are destroyed with a great and terrible destruction.

Bible Teaching

The passage can be divided into two parts: first, the account of Zacchaeus and second, the parable of the minas.

◀ 19:1-10. It is important to notice that Zacchaeus is a tax collector. Their standing in the culture of Jesus' day has already been described in chapter 13 of this study, dealing with the calling of Levi. These men were hated. But to make matters worse, Zacchaeus was a *chief* tax collector. He had excelled in his profession and had become wealthy by exploiting his countrymen. If an ordinary tax collector was hated, Zacchaeus as their chief would be despised all the more (v. 7). Yet even this vile offender is precious in God's sight. As a result of Jesus' visit to his house, he repents in word and action by restoring what he had wrongfully taken. These are fruits of a changed heart, and Jesus acknowledges his repentance and, like the Prodigal Son, welcomes him again to the family of Abraham. Though the Jews would not accept him as their brother, Jesus fully restores Zacchaeus to the family of the faith.

◀ 19:11-27. The parable of the minas concerns a nobleman who is about to be made king. However, some of his subjects do not love him and would have him vanquished from his newly acquired throne. Ten servants are given a mina each, not a large sum, to manage in his absence. Most of these men diligently serve their king so that, when he returns, one has increased his mina tenfold and another fivefold. There is one servant who does not work with his mina. His mina is taken from him and given to another. So it is with the Israelites who, knowing the King, refuse to serve Him. The Pharisees are like this unfaithful servant in rejecting Jesus' rule in His heavenly kingdom. Their place in the kingdom is taken and given to another. Though they think themselves more significant than the tax collector in God's economy, the tax collector bears fruit in keeping with repentance. Therefore he will be blessed, but they will be subjected to the severest punishment of the king, even slaughter.

Family Discussion

Talk about the importance of bearing fruit no matter when you start.

Little Children: Talk about how God entrusts them with talents and possessions. Show that, out of gratitude for Christ's salvation, they should use these to serve the Lord.

Middle Children: Show your children the progression of a changed life. First, Jesus calls Zacchaeus, then he repents. In the second parable, the king assigns the task first and then his servants work. Talk about the importance of that order.

Older Children: Discuss the severity of the punishment of those enemies who rejected the king's rule: they were slaughtered. How does this statement compare with popular focus on Jesus' mercy at the expense of His justice? Talk about fear of judgment as a proper motivation for serving the Lord.

Family Singing

Great King of Nations, Hear Our Prayer (Trinity Hymnal #713); Why Do Gentile Nations Rage (Psalter #2B)

Family Prayer

Ask the Lord to help you bear fruit in keeping with repentance. Pray for those you know who are currently enemies of Christ.

CHAPTER 49

The Triumphal Entry

TODAY'S READING: LUKE 19:28-48.

Introduction

Jesus arrives at Jerusalem amidst great celebration. The people usher Him into Jerusalem as a hero with the expectation that He will restore the kingdom of David. However, Jesus does not enter Jerusalem to establish an earthly kingdom. When He arrives in the temple He teaches about His spiritual kingdom.

Bible Teaching

These verses can be divided into the entry into Jerusalem, Jesus' sorrow over Jerusalem, and the events that lead the priests and scribes to seek to destroy Him.

◀ 19:28-40. Jesus enters Jerusalem on a colt, a sign of a kingdom at peace. From Matthew's parallel account we know this entry was the fulfillment of Old Testament prophecy (cf. Zech. 9:9). The miraculous way His disciples obtain this colt show His prophetic office. He sends His disciples to fetch the beast, predicting a strange series of events which take place according to His prediction. As He sits on the colt, the accompanying crowd praises God. They called Christ the King who comes in the name of the Lord, a citation from Psalm 118:26. Their words are actually true, though their intended application of them in an earthy kingdom are not correct. However, Jesus does not silence them. The words are true and should be properly applied to Christ.

◀ 19:41-44. Contrary to the crowd's expectation of an earthly kingdom, Jesus has not come to establish one. Instead, He predicts David's city will soon be destroyed. The things needed for peace, which are spiritual in nature, are hidden from the eyes of the worldly minded. Jerusalem's destruction will be so complete, not even two stones will remain one upon another. If there is no capital city, there can be no kingdom. Jesus did not come to be respected in Jerusalem, but to be rejected there.[1] He, in turn, rejects the city though He does it with weeping.

---

1. Matthew Henry, *Matthew Henry's Commentary on the Whole Bible*, Volume 3 (Grand Rapids, MI: Guardian Press, 1976), 456.

◀ 19:45-48. Instead of zeal for the earthly kingdom, Jesus shows His love for His Heavenly Father, a mark of every citizen of heaven. He enters the temple and drives out those who would abuse the worship of God for selfish profit. This action does not escape the notice of the priests and other influential men. Even as Jesus teaches them in the temple, their hearts are veiled and they seek Jesus' destruction. Their plans are delayed for a short time as they seek to sway the masses to support them.

Family Discussion

Talk about the importance of seeking your deliverance on a spiritual plane, not a physical.

Little Children: Talk about Jesus as the King who comes in the name of the Lord (v. 38). What kingdom did the Father send the Son to take over? Show how Jesus did not come to establish an earthly kingdom but to call them to be subjects in His heavenly kingdom.

Middle Children: Look at the fulfillments of prophecy about Jesus in this passage. See Zechariah 9:9 and Psalm 118:26. Talk about Jesus' fulfillment of prophecy as clear evidence of who He is. Show how He did not come on His own initiative but was sent by the Father to be the perfect Passover Lamb (cf. 1 Cor. 5:7).

Older Children: Look at the statement of Jesus in verse 46. Think about some ways people may use Christianity for their own advantage today. Discuss the purpose of worship as never being centered on man, but always directed toward the Lord in response to the work of Christ.

Family Singing

Come Thou Long Expected Jesus (Trinity Hymnal #196); That Man Is Blessed (Psalter #1A)

Family Prayer

Ask the Lord to help you worship Him in His spiritual kingdom. Ask Him to keep you from making His house a den of robbers.

CHAPTER 50

Jesus' Authority

TODAY'S READING: LUKE 20:1-26.

Introduction

In today's passage the religious leaders reject Jesus' authority, seeking to discredit Him through insincere questions. However, Jesus, as the Heir from the Father, holds true authority. Even the greatest rulers of this world are of no consequence to Him. They can have their gold coins. His authority demands something far greater than a few gold coins.

Bible Teaching

We can progress through this passage in three separate stages, each adding to the teaching on Jesus' authority:

◀ 20:1-8. This first section introduces the question of authority. The priests try to discredit Jesus' authority in front of the people. Questioning God's authority is first seen in Satan's initial temptation to Eve in the Garden of Eden, as well. Here, the Jewish leaders use that tactic regarding Jesus' teaching as He instructs in the temple (v. 47). Their question would be a good one if asked in sincerity because the answer would affirm Christ's divinity and His special status as God's Son. However, the motive behind the question is bad, so Jesus does not entrust them with His answer. Instead He exposes their hypocrisy by forcing them to take one of two unpopular positions should they answer His question. For the religious leaders, human approval is more important than the truth, and so the question remains unanswered.

◀ 20:9-18. What is not answered by the religious leaders, Jesus answers in the parable that follows. A landowner sends messengers to collect his share of the fruit. These messengers, representing the prophets of Israel, are beaten and sent away empty-handed. When the owner sends his son, they threw him out and killed him. The priests understand the implication of this parable and react when Jesus says the vineyard will be given to others. Jesus, quoting from Psalm 118:22, warns them about their rejection of Him, the cornerstone. This stone will either encourage broken sinners to cast themselves on Christ or crush them.

◀ 20:19-26. Finally we see an example of Jesus' authority. The priests are consumed with trying to shame Christ. Their preference would be to 'lay hands on him,' but they are afraid to do so because of the people. Instead they try to win the people over by asking Jesus a question about taxes. If Jesus answers they should not pay taxes, they could complain to the Romans; if He answers they should pay taxes, the people would despise Him. However, Jesus' answer shows the insignificance of those little coins. Essentially He says, 'Let Caesar have his little golden pieces, but give to God what is owed to Him: worship and obedience to His authority.'

Family Discussion
Work through the importance of Jesus' authority as it relates to our relationship with Him.

Little Children: Talk about authority and ask if they know what authority is. Show how everyone is to obey Jesus because He is everyone's authority.

Middle Children: Look at the parable of the tenants in its different parts. Talk about the servants as the prophets and show how they were treated badly (cf. 1 Kings 19:2; 22:26). Who are the current tenants, and to whom will the vineyard be given? Who is the heir?

Older Children: Talk about the dishonesty in the religious leaders' question about taxes. Talk about those who are hardened in unbelief and how they do not desire, nor are they able, to hear the truth. How does Jesus' answer turn us away from this life toward obedience to God? What does it mean to render to God the things that are God's?

Family Singing
The Church's One Foundation (Trinity Hymnal #347); Your Word's a Lamp (Psalter #119N)

Family Prayer
Thank God for His Word and ask Him to give you humble hearts as you respond to His authority.

CHAPTER 51

Jesus Condemns the Sadducees

TODAY'S READING: LUKE 20:27-21:4.

Introduction

The Sadducees test Jesus intending to defame Him. In dealing with their question, Jesus proves them inadequate spiritual leaders of the people. In the presence of the people, Jesus warns these men about their fate.

Bible Teaching

The initial question regarding the resurrection takes up most of the verses today. However, Jesus moves beyond this question to show the Sadducees' ineptitude in handling the Word and to give them a stern warning.

◀ 20:27-40. The Sadducees were members of the Jewish ruling class who rejected the resurrection (cf. Acts 23:8). With that in mind, the Sadducees come to Jesus to test Him with, what they thought to be, an unanswerable question. The question involves the Old Testament laws where a dead man's brother was to take his widow as his wife to continue his dead brother's name (cf. Deut. 25:5-6), also known as levirate marriages. The Sadducees thought this law created an inconsistency if there was a resurrection. If seven brothers all marry the same woman, what will happen at the resurrection? The implication is that 'real life' creates so many problems for how things will work in the resurrection that the whole proposition is ludicrous. Jesus rebukes them, showing they are missing the point of the story of redemption in the Bible. Christ has come to reverse the effects of sin and death, according to what is written in Scripture. There is a resurrection as can be seen in Moses' calling God the God of the patriarchs, who had long since been buried (cf. Exod. 3:6). By denying the resurrection the Sadducees show they are not able to understand God's Word.

◀ 20:41-44. Jesus continues to press them, showing their complete lack of understanding of the Bible, even when it comes to the Messiah. They are looking for David's son, but in reality the One who is coming is David's Lord. The Messiah will not be subservient to David, but is exalted over him. He will rule over a greater kingdom and exercise greater power in His reign. The religious leaders had missed this theological fact altogether by hoping for the reinstitution of the Davidic monarchy.

◀ 20:45-21:4. Finally, Jesus warns the people of the scribes' motives. Their religion is not sincere but they have a hidden agenda. They desire to be publically recognized and honored by men. They may have their itches scratched here on earth, but in the final analysis they will face greater condemnation before God. The scribes have surrendered nothing of themselves to God. By contrast the poor widow gives all she has to the Lord. It is in her sacrificial service to the Lord that true worship is found.

Family Discussion
Talk about the significance of the resurrection.

Little Children: Look at Genesis 2:17 to see how death entered the world through sin. If death is caused by sin, what does it mean when death is no more? Talk about how Christ takes away all the sins of His people so they will be free from death.

Middle Children: Look at John 11:25 and talk about the significance of Jesus' identity as the resurrection. If Jesus was not raised from the dead could He really be our Savior? Discuss the significance of Jesus breaking the power of the grave.

Older Children: Talk about the complete surrender to God of the widow. Show how external obedience alone is inadequate, but that our works should be the works of a resurrected soul.

Family Singing
How Firm a Foundation (Trinity Hymnal #94); My Portion Is the Lord (Psalter #119H)

Family Prayer
Ask God to teach you to come to His Word humbly, willing to change your life in the face of His promises and commands.

CHAPTER 52

Ominous Signs

TODAY'S READING: LUKE 21:5-24.

Introduction

The temple was immensely significant for the people of Israel. It seems their esteem for God's temple had even become idolatrous. However, the temple is only significant as it represents God's presence with His people. Jesus teaches the manifestations of God's presence will soon change as the physical buildings will be destroyed.

Bible Teaching

To teach this idea, Jesus predictively speaks of the destruction of Jerusalem and the temple in A.D. 70. There is the warning of the destruction of the temple, the presence of geopolitical turmoil, and the destruction of Jerusalem.

◀21:5-9. The disciples stand in awe of the temple. But Jesus corrects His disciples regarding their esteem for buildings. Their confidence is misplaced because buildings pass away. The temple was always intended to point forward to Christ Himself. As Solomon's temple was destroyed in 586 B.C., so also the temple of Herod will be completely destroyed in A.D. 70. As recorded in Josephus' *History of the Jewish War*, the temple was destroyed by Titus, the son of emperor Vespasian, whose soldiers burned the temple to the ground. The center of Israel's sacrificial system was razed never to be rebuilt. This destruction was an ominous sign of judgment to come.

◀21:10-18. There are other indications of the coming judgment. Jesus speaks of the great hardships God's people will endure. Even today many brothers and sisters continue to face these hardships. Persecutions, imprisonments, betrayal, and martyrdom await Jesus' disciples. These descriptions may seem at odds with Jesus' promise of preservation (v. 18), but only if the eternal redemption purchased for the Christian through which their salvation is assured into eternity is ignored. Because of redemption accomplished by Christ for His disciples, 'some of them shall lose their heads, and yet not lose a hair!'[1]

---

1. Matthew Henry, 463.

◀21:19-24. Jesus continues to warn, speaking of the destruction of Jerusalem. This destruction involved horrendous and grotesque abuse. The abuse would not only come at the hands of the Romans, but also from the Jewish rebels, the Zealots. It is estimated nearly one million Jews died during the siege in A.D. 70. Jesus grieves over this destruction, a result of the sin of the people of Israel for which they are entirely responsible.

Family Discussion

Work through the justice of God in administering punishment on those who rebel against Him.

Little Children: Explain to your children that one of the motives for discipline is to warn them to change their behavior and to seek forgiveness. Talk to them about how Jesus warns people to turn to Him because He does not want them to be destroyed.

Middle Children: Talk about how the destruction of the temple as the center of Jewish worship prepares the world for the universal church. Talk about how the destruction of Jerusalem takes away the Jewish political center yet prepares them for a spiritual kingdom.

Older Children: Talk about the significance of persecution in the life of the believer. Talk about whether they are ready to be persecuted for the faith. In the October 1, 2015, shootings at Umpqua Community College in Oregon, the gunman asked his victims if they were Christians or not. If they answered yes, he shot them in the head. How would they face such a question?

Family Singing

O for a Thousand Tongues to Sing (Trinity Hymnal #164); Who with God Most High Finds Shelter (Psalter #91A)

Family Prayer

Ask the Lord to grant you strength in persecution and thank Him for including the Gentiles among the people of God.

CHAPTER 53

Christ's Return

TODAY'S READING: LUKE 21:25-38.

Introduction

In today's verses Jesus addresses His second coming. The return of Christ will be the only part of God's plan of redemption left undone after His ascension. In speaking of His return, Jesus uses a high degree of symbolic language. Yet that to which these words point is as certain as the ground on which Jesus and His disciples walked. The signs call for repentance and avoidance of God's final judgment against sin.

Bible Teaching

Jesus first speaks of His return, then gives an illustration, and finally warns His listeners.

◀ 21:25-28. The signs in sun, moon, and stars are hyperbolic. This picture of the destruction of the heavenly lights is also used in some of the prophets (cf. Isa. 13:10; Joel 2:10). The point is not about the sun and the stars, but rather the dread that will accompany that time. Everything we count on for stability will be shaken before our eyes. These things will cause great distress yet are not the final judgment itself. There is one final sign that reveals the impending doom for the godless, namely Christ's second coming. For God's people, Christ's appearance is good news. Their redemption is about to be perfected and completed.

◀ 21:29-36. These events give a general understanding of where we are in the timeline of redemption. The 'these things' of verse 31 relate back to verse 20 and the destruction of Jerusalem and departure of the saints. They are a sign that the season of Christ's return is imminent and will be witnessed even by the present generation. The exact timing of His return is not known (v. 34), but these events teach there is nothing left to be accomplished in redemption before His return. Therefore man should remain watchful and guard his heart. Appealing to God for strength, the people of God are called to persevere (v. 36).

◀ 21:37-38. Even in His last days, Jesus did all He could to warn the people of Jerusalem of the pending doom. He taught them daily in the temple. Yet

Christ so conceals His glory and majesty in His humiliation on earth that He does not demand splendor for Himself. The nights He spends on a mountain, returning to the temple each morning to declare the glorious good news: that those who trust in Him would be spared from the coming wrath.

Family Discussion

Talk about the good news of salvation that keeps you from having to face God's judgment.

Little Children: Talk about what happens when Jesus comes again. Show them the joy of heaven (cf. Rev. 21:1-4). Also touch on the judgment of the wicked and those who would not serve Christ. Talk about faith in Christ and the hope they have through it.

Middle Children: Talk about Christ's imminent return. Show how all parts of the promise of God have been fulfilled save one: the second coming. Talk about how Christ's return glorifies God since every knee will bow before Him.

Older Children: Talk about the 'fairness' of God's judgment. Why is it fair that God condemns some and saves others? Talk about the perspective of the world that would charge God with not being fair in condemning people. Show how this thought assumes the goodness of man. Instead impress on your teens that God's mercy is seen in that He spares any since all have sinned against Him.

Family Singing

Joy to the World, the Lord Is Come (Trinity Hymnal #195); All, Like Mount Zion, Unmoved Shall Endure (Psalter #125)

Family Prayer

Ask the Lord to spare specific friends or family members from the judgment to come. Thank Him for salvation in Christ.

CHAPTER 54

Jesus' Last Meal

TODAY'S READING: LUKE 22:1-23.

Introduction

As the Passover approaches, the priests begin to seek a way to put Jesus to death. The only reason they hesitate is because the people hold Him in high regard. Even as Jesus prepares His disciples for His departure by instituting the sacrament of the Lord's Supper, Judas conspires with the religious leaders to hand Jesus over to them.

Bible Teaching

The plot of Jesus' betrayal introduces the final measures Jesus takes to prepare His disciples.

◀ 22:1-6. The religious leaders' hatred for Jesus has made them willing to kill Him. Their hatred is not based on any sin they thought He committed. If so, the crowd could be convinced through a regular, public trial. However, the need for secrecy shows their grievance against Jesus is personal. They are not concerned with God's Law but with their own positions of power. Unable to find a way to execute their plans, Judas comes to their aid. Perhaps he has grown disillusioned with Jesus. For whatever reason, Satan had entered his heart (cf. John 13:27). He approaches the religious leaders, who gladly pay him to provide the opportunity to arrest Jesus in secret.

◀ 22:7-13. The first day of the Passover festival, a Thursday, Jesus prepares for His own sacrifice with His disciples. There is a miraculous element to the preparations, just as in the triumphal entry. We should not speculate about the roles of the different men or the significance of the man carrying the water. These things are not explained for us in Scripture. What is significant, however, is that the disciples find the arrangements exactly as Jesus predicted. The Messiah, fully God and fully man, has come to take away the sin of the world, and the climax of His ministry has begun.

◀ 22:14-23. The institution of the Lord's Supper, teaches several things. First, the Old Testament shadow of the Passover finds New Testament fulfillment.

The perfect Passover Lamb's blood (cf. 1 Cor. 5:7) will be painted on the doorposts of His people's hearts so the angel of destruction might pass over. Second, the bread and wine symbolize Christ's work on the Cross. When Jesus held the bread and said, 'This is my body,' the disciples did not think He was holding His actual flesh. The bread and wine only represented His body and blood. Third, the institution of the Lord's Supper demonstrates that not all who partake of the meal are forgiven. Judas ate and woe is pronounced on him.

Family Discussion

Talk about the sacrifice of Christ to your family and set before them the greatness of it.

Little Children: Remind your children that the wages of sin is death. Talk to them about how Jesus dies in their place so they do not face this death themselves. Talk about the joy of the resurrection for those who believe God's promises.

Middle Children: Talk about the significance of the Passover as a remembrance of Israel's deliverance from Egypt. Show the deliverance from sin by Christ. How are Christ's blood and the Passover lamb's blood of the Old Testament similar? How are they different?

Older Children: Talk about the Lord's Supper as a memorial meal. Talk about how God communicates grace to those who partake by faith. Show how He strengthens their faith, draws them closer to Himself, and deepens their love for Him through the Supper just as He does in those who read His Word by faith.

Family Singing

Christ, Whose Glory Fills the Sky (Trinity Hymnal #398); God Is Our Refuge and Our Strength (Psalter #46B)

Family Prayer

Thank God for sending Christ to be our Passover Lamb. Ask for help to remember His body was broken and His blood was shed for you.

CHAPTER 55

The Prayer of the Savior

TODAY'S READING: LUKE 22:24-53.

Introduction

Jesus spends His last night before the crucifixion talking with His disciples and praying. They need this instruction since they are still struggling to properly understand Jesus' ministry. The temptation of the physical power of the sword is still strong in these men, yet Jesus will submit Himself peacefully to His executioners that He might fulfill the purpose for which the Father sent Him.

Bible Teaching

The verses today show a contrast between the disciples' desire to fight and Jesus' peaceful submission to His Father's will.

◀ 22:24-34. As soon as the disciples leave the upper room they begin to argue about who will be most significant. From John's Gospel we know Jesus has just washed his disciples' feet demonstrating they must serve each other (cf. John 13:1-17), yet their primary concern is their own status. Jesus reminds them they must be servants (v. 27). However highly the disciples may think of themselves, they must know their weak nature. Peter is singled out and his denial of Christ is predicted. Despite his previous confession of Jesus as the Christ (cf. Luke 9:20), he will deny even knowing Jesus (v. 34). It is the ultimate manifestation that man's flesh is not reliable.

◀ 22:35-46. Next Jesus shows His disciples their relationship with the world is about to change. Jesus will no longer be with them to supply their needs in the same way. They will begin to execute His mission without His physical presence. The disciples take this teaching to mean they must arm themselves for a physical battle, the error of which is not shown to them until Jesus' arrest. Because of the significance of these verses the next chapter will deal with other implications. For the consideration on prayer, it is shown as the proper weapon for Christian disciples. Jesus models its proper use in His moment of great anguish. Despite His own desires, Jesus places His Father's desires first (v. 42). The disciples sought their will, yet Jesus shows them how to seek the Father's will first.

◀ 22:47-53. Judas leads an armed crowd (cf. Matt. 26:47), having arranged a secret signal of a kiss to mark who they should arrest. Peter strikes the ear of the servant of the high priest with his sword. However, Jesus rebukes them and heals the man's ear. He also confronts the cowardice of the chief priests who come in darkness to arrest Him. They come at night because they belong to the night. Yet Jesus is at peace and does not resist. He has come to do His Father's will.

Family Discussion

Talk about the importance of seeking the Lord's will first.

Little Children: Look at Philippians 2:4 and compare how the disciples live to how Jesus lives. Talk about Jesus' desire to follow His Father. Talk about wordliness as a preoccupation with this world and its supposed pleasures.

Middle Children: Talk about the objects of the disciples' trust. Explain how their preoccupation with their position and reliance on swords show they have not understood the spiritual nature of Christ's work. Look at verse 42 to show the appropriate contrast in Christ.

Older Children: From verse 42, discuss how Christ's perfect will is different from man's sinful will. Talk about the Son's faithfulness to the plan of redemption in fulfilling all the Father sent Him to do. Discuss how our own lives and prayers should be shaped in the same way (cf. Eph. 5:1).

Family Singing

O the Deep, Deep Love of Jesus (Trinity Hymnal #535); Bless the Lord, My Soul (Psalter #103B)

Family Prayer

Ask the Lord to keep you from trusting the strength of men but to lean on the Lord instead.

CHAPTER 56

Christic Our Willing Substitute

CHAPTER 56

Christ Our Willing Substitute

TODAY'S READING: LUKE 22:39-53.

Introduction

Jesus' prayer and betrayal in Gethsemane show much of the Trinitarian work of redemption. The Son yields to the Father's will, not because He is a less significant person in the Godhead. He willingly does all His Father's will out of His love for His Father and His people, knowing this course will lead to their redemption and the conquering of the power of darkness.

Bible Teaching

Christ's willingness to suffer and die is first seen in His prayers on the Mount of Olives and subsequently in His words and actions during His arrest by the chief priests and their band.

◄ 22:39-46. As Jesus' death approaches, the agony of His crucifixion weighs on Him. Christ is facing something far more formidable than a simple apprehension about death. Many people have faced circumstances in which they can see their death coming and have not reacted with sweating great drops of blood (v. 44). Instead, Christ faces the reality of bearing the wrath of God. Though He may struggle with this part of His earthly ministry, He does not rebel against God. He is like us in every way, except for sin. Christ does ask for His cup to be taken from Him (v. 42), but this question is properly qualified by His desire to do the Father's will first. His love for His people is such that He willingly suffers the cross to pay the debt of their sin. He asks God for relief, but not in such a way as to indicate any unwillingness on His part. Rather, He obeys the will of God freely, and without reservation.

◄ 22:47-53. When Jesus is handed over to the chief priests it is by one of His closest friends, Judas Iscariot. Though Judas thinks his intentions well disguised by his kiss, Jesus knows Judas desires to betray Him. Christ experiences the betrayal of those closest to Him. Yet, when the disciples suggest they overpower the arresting band by force, Jesus knows the Father's will must be followed. When the high priest's servant's ear is cut off, Jesus heals him. Jesus goes willingly with His captors. Though Judas

126

and the religious rulers think their moment of victory has come, Jesus says it is only an hour (v. 53), showing His confidence in God's final victory.

Family Discussion

The willingness of Christ to serve as our substitute makes His gift so much greater than if He were forced to die on the Cross.

Little Children: Talk to your children about the difference between being forced to share a toy compared to willingly doing so. In which instance are they happier about their action? Talk about how Christ willingly suffers and dies for their sins and how this shows His love for them is very great.

Middle Children: Talk about the difference between asking God to remove a trial and rebelling against Him. Show how Jesus' desire is to submit to the Father (v. 12). Talk about how Jesus is not an inferior person in the Trinity, but equal to the Father in substance and glory. Talk about their difference being one of function in redemption, not in essence of person.

Older Children: Study Christ's agony in Gethsemane in light of Isaiah 53:6; Galatians 3:13; and 1 Peter 2:22-24. Discuss how this part of Jesus' ministry would weigh on Him more now as He approaches the hour of its actual experience. Discuss the greatness of God's love seen in the work of redemption.

Family Singing

O the Deep, Deep Love of Jesus (Trinity Hymnal #535); Bless the Lord, My Soul (Psalter #103B)

Family Prayer

Spend time in prayer thanking God for His work of redemption and all that He suffered on account of our sins.

CHAPTER 57

Kangaroo Court

Introduction

Under the cover of darkness, the Pharisees take Jesus to the high priest's house for a mock trial. The disciples have all abandoned Jesus, except for Peter and John. Far from being a comfort to Christ, Peter denies he even knows Him. But Jesus, knowing His time has come, professes the truth about who He is. Instead of glorifying the Creator, His creation rejects Him and sentences Him to death.

Bible Teaching

Peter's denial, the soldiers, and the priests all intensify Christ's humiliation on earth, which is accentuated here with His final sentencing.

◀ 22:54-62. Peter's denial is both devastating and comforting. It is devastating on several levels. First, to see a fellow disciple's frailty so clearly recorded is disconcerting. Second, the emotional pain this denial must have caused Christ is tragic. Imagine being unjustly sentenced to die and even your best friend is not willing to stand with you. Third, we see the disgrace of Peter. Somehow, after the third denial, Jesus is able to look directly into the eyes of the one who swore he would even go to the grave for Him (cf. Matt. 26:35). Peter's shame is immediate and drives him to tears (v. 62). But this section of Scripture is also greatly comforting because we know that Peter is later reinstated (cf. John 21:15-19). He is given the special privilege of being an apostle. His sin is not held against him, but God accepts his repentance.

◀ 22:63-65. Yet not everyone who denies Christ will turn from their sin. His captors who came in cowardice under the cover of night now use this same cover to blaspheme the very One who made them. They blindfold, beat, and mock Him. There is no repentance among them. It seems like Satan has emerged victorious.

◀ 22:66-71. Christ is not dismayed in the presence of these foes. No longer does He answer their questions with questions. Instead He professes what they were hoping He would say: He is the Son of the Most High. His identity, which caused demons to plead with Him (cf. Luke 8:28), infuriates these hardened men. They consider his words blasphemous. If Jesus' claim was made by any other man, their outrage would be justified. However, it is not blasphemous for God to say He is God. Notwithstanding His innocence, Jesus is handed over to the Roman governor Pilate by the Jewish religious leaders who hope to pressure the governor to carry out a capital sentence against Him.

Family Discussion

Talk about Jesus' suffering, specifically as it is experienced in this unjust sentence handed down against the very God of creation.

Little Children: Talk about when they are disciplined. Ask them to give you some examples of ways in which they sinned and had to be corrected. Ask them if Jesus ever committed any sin. Show them that He was punished not for His own sin but for their sin.

Middle Children: Talk about Peter's denial and how his objective was to preserve himself. Talk about the great anguish that must have been in his heart (v. 62), but also show the great comfort of his restoration (cf. John 21:15-19).

Older Children: Talk about Christ's sinlessness, even in His trial (cf. 1 Pet. 2:22-24). Show how the basis of the charge of the priests does not rest on truth but on their own rejection of the truth. Make sure they understand the significance of the sinlessness of Christ.

Family Singing

The Church's One Foundation (Trinity Hymnal #347); My Portion is the Lord (Psalter #119H)

Family Prayer

Ask the Lord to make you bold professors of your faith in Him even in circumstances where we are under pressure to deny Him.

CHAPTER 58

In the Hands of the Romans

TODAY'S READING: LUKE 23:1-25.

Introduction

The Jews have made their decision about Jesus' guilt, but His case must be adjudicated legally. If He is to assume His people's legal penalty, He must be tried in a legal setting, not dispatched by a mob. Jesus is sent to Pilate and Herod to be condemned. However, the wickedness of these men is the vehicle God uses to accomplish redemption. The crucifixion of Christ makes salvation a reality.

Bible Teaching

The legal sentencing of Jesus begins with the Roman governor, Pilate, and moves to Herod. Despite knowing Him to be an innocent man, they still condemn Him to die to serve their own political purposes. But they really are serving God's sovereign plan of redemption through Christ.

◀ 23:1-5. Satisfied they had found enough justification for the death penalty under Jewish Law, the leaders take Jesus to Pilate because they are not permitted to execute a man (cf. John 18:31). Once in Pilate's presence, notice their charges against Jesus change from blasphemy to sedition. Even in their charges, the priests and scribes are untruthful. They have adopted the language of their father, the devil, who is the father of lies. When Pilate's initial interview with Jesus does not provide any evidence that He is a guilty man, the Jews insist He is stirring up rebellion from Galilee to Judea. Pilate, who would like nothing better than to rid himself of this case, assigns it to Herod, the tetrarch of that region.

◀ 23:6-12. Herod was glad to receive Jesus because he hoped to see some kind of spectacle. When none is forthcoming, the tetrarch satisfies himself with mocking Jesus instead. He dresses the prisoner in splendid clothes and sends Him back to Pilate. This public mockery of Christ becomes the foundation for Herod and Pilate's new friendship, an illustration of Psalm 2:1-3.

◀ 23:13-25. Upon His return to Pilate's court, the Roman governor makes some effort to free Jesus because he believes Him innocent. However, in the end he gives in to the demand of the crowd. A proper legal judge pronounces a capital sentence against a man he knows to be innocent, sending Him to one of the most agonizing deaths man has ever invented. In exchange he releases to the Jews a man who is known as an insurrectionist. Ironically, the Jews falsely accused Jesus of being a dissenter against the Roman authorities before Pilate, yet Barabbas, who truly is an insurrectionist, is released to them.

Family Discussion

Talk about Jesus' sinless life and His enduring the injustice of His conviction.

Little Children: Talk about judges and how people are sentenced when they have done something wrong. Next show them how Jesus, though He never sinned, was condemned to death. Ask them if they know why Jesus died, and talk about His sacrifice for sinful men.

Middle Children: Talk about the wickedness of the Jewish leaders of Jesus' time and show how they changed their story about Jesus from blasphemy to sedition. Talk about how God uses the sins of Jewish leaders to accomplish the cornerstone of the redemption of His people (cf. Acts 2:23).

Older Children: Talk about the injustice of the legal sentence handed down on Jesus. Show how Jesus, as Mediator, submits Himself to this unjust sentence so His people may be forgiven. Show how Satan is only a pawn in God's plan of redemption, though he thinks he is victorious. Discuss the great love of God in the work of redemption (cf. Rom. 8:32).

Family Singing

Christ Whose Glory Fills the Sky (Trinity Hymnal #398); O All You Nations of the Earth (Psalter #117A)

Family Prayer

Thank the Lord for suffering in your place. Thank Him for His plan of salvation.

CHAPTER 59

The Death of the Savior

TODAY'S READING: LUKE 23:26-56.

Introduction

Many things at Jesus' death confirm the significance of the occasion. The mercy of Christ, even in His agony, is astounding. Although even His mockers realize the shame of what they had done, they do not demonstrate faith in Christ or repentance over sin.

Bible Teaching

Today's verses can be divided into Jesus' death, its significance, and the faithful actions of Joseph of Arimathea.

◀ 23:26-43. The crowds following Jesus to Golgotha either mocked or mourned. Even in His agony Jesus sought to comfort the mourners. The dividing of His garments (cf. Ps. 22:18) and the words of the crowd (cf. Ps. 22:8) fulfill Old Testament prophecies about Christ. The overall tenor of the mob is one of mockery. The leaders, soldiers, and even the criminals crucified next to Him mock Him (cf. Matt. 27:44). Yet Jesus shows His mercy when one of the mocking criminals repents (v. 41). The man demonstrates a sure knowledge of Christ and true faith in Him. His desire to enter Christ's kingdom must refer to a spiritual kingdom since a crucified man had no hope of entering anything in this world (v. 42). He entrusts himself to this newly understood promise, and Jesus grants him redemption.

◀ 23:44-49. Many of the events surrounding Jesus' death show its significance. First, the sun yields her light to her Creator as He dies. The normal created order is interrupted as the Son of God becomes the recipient of God's wrath for man's sin. At Jesus' death everything became dark from noon to 3 p.m. Second, the curtain in the temple was torn from top to bottom (v. 45). This curtain maintained the distance between God and man, but now the Son's sacrifice was complete the separation was removed by God Himself as indicated by the tearing happening from top to bottom. No man could have divided the curtain in this way. Through Christ's death, man is reconciled to God. Finally, Jesus willingly surrenders His spirit, which makes even a hardened centurion recognize Jesus' innocence. The voluntary nature of Jesus' sacrifice is manifested. He was a voluntary participant, even to the point of death. These events sent even the mockers home in shame, though without any true repentance.

◀ 23:50-56. Only some among the crowd demonstrate faith in action. Only the thief and Joseph of Arimathea honor Christ. Immediately following Jesus' death, the latter does what he can to prepare Jesus' body for burial placing Him in his own tomb. Amazingly, the disciples leave Jesus' body unattended until Sunday, leaving Saturday for rest in honor of the Sabbath.

Family Discussion
Discuss the significance of Jesus' death.

Little Children: Talk about Jesus dying on the Cross. From Genesis 2:17 show them how they should die because of sin, but that Jesus did not have to because He did not sin. Talk about Jesus dying in their place as their substitute.

Middle Children: Talk about the criminal's repentance. Show how his comment about entering His kingdom (v. 42) demonstrates true faith. Discuss how his conversion was more than simple convenience. Discuss the importance of coming to faith.

Older Children: Look at the circumstances surrounding Jesus' death: the darkness, tearing of the curtain, and His voluntary surrender of His spirit. Specifically talk about the tearing of the curtain in light of Exodus 26:31ff and how redemption accomplished by Christ replaces the annual work of the high priest on the Day of Atonement (cf. Lev. 16).

Family Singing
Come Thou Long-Expected Jesus (Trinity Hymnal #196); Why Do Gentile Nations Rage (Psalter #2B)

Family Prayer
Thank God for His plan of redemption. Ask Him to give you a sense of awe over what He has done for sinners.

CHAPTER 60

Redemption's Accomplishment Guaranteed

TODAY'S READING: LUKE 24:1-12.

Introduction

Jesus' death would have been in vain had He not been raised from the dead. It would have shown that sin's penalty had not been paid since its effects would be seen in Him. Certain women, who had followed Him from Galilee, meet the angels at the empty tomb. These heavenly messengers instruct the women to tell the disciples what they had seen. Through these events, the disciples begin to understand the significance of Jesus' resurrection.

Bible Teaching

This passage flows from the angel's interaction with the women, to the disciples' doubting response, and finally to the few who began to see the fulfillment of God's promise of redemption.

◀ 24:1-7. Early in the morning, on the first day of the week, the women go to the tomb. After spending Friday night, Saturday, and Sunday morning in the grave, Jesus is raised from the dead. In Luke's account there are two angels. Matthew and Mark speak of one angel, but do not exclude the possibility of two. The angels reassure the trembling women and remind them of Jesus' prediction of His resurrection (cf. Luke 9:21-22). Armed with this information, the women are sent to tell the other disciples to meet Jesus in Galilee (cf. Matt. 28:7; Mark 16:7).

◀ 24:8-11. Returning from the tomb, the women tell the other disciples of their experience at the tomb. However, the men think it was just a crazy story. Their minds are still anchored in the things of this world. How marvelous is God's patience and long-suffering with His people. They had not yet been given full understanding and belief by the Holy Spirit, yet the seed of belief is beginning to sprout. This blossoming faith can be seen in Peter's reaction to the news.

◀ 24:12. From John 20:3, we know that Peter did not go alone, but in Luke, only Peter's visit to the empty tomb is recorded. He runs to verify the report of the women. His reaction manifests his faith. He must have believed the report enough to see whether it was true or not, but here the significance of Christ's work is beginning to be seen more clearly by him. As he sees the empty tomb, he marvels at what had happened. Peter realizes the resurrection has occurred. Its full meaning was not yet clear to him, but God, in His grace, was beginning to work in His disciples.

Family Discussion

Talk about the centrality of the resurrection for the guarantee that Jesus' death paid for the debt of sin.

Little Children: Ask your children if they believe you when you make a promise. Talk about the Bible as God's promise. Talk to them about how they can also believe the accounts about Jesus because the people who gave or recorded the accounts saw what happened.

Middle Children: Talk about Peter's faith. He heard the women's words and believed, at least to some extent. Talk about how they also hear the account of the resurrection and must respond in faith. Talk about the resurrection as a reversal of the consequence of the Fall.

Older Children: Considering 1 Corinthians 15:19, talk about the significance of the resurrection as a sign that the effect of sin was reversed. With death entering the world through sin (cf. 1 Cor. 15:21), talk about the importance of Jesus' victory over death in His resurrection. Show how, if Jesus had remained dead, it would demonstrate He had been a sinner and therefore unable to pay our debt.

Family Singing

How Firm a Foundation (Trinity Hymnal #94); Your Word's a Lamp (Psalter #119N)

Family Prayer

Praise God for the resurrection and His work of atonement. Thank Him for telling us about the resurrection in His Word.

CHAPTER 61

Faith on the Rise

Introduction

On the Road to Emmaus a very important biblical connection is made between the Old Testament and Christ. The Bible is one book with one subject. It is an account of God's plan of redemption accomplished by our Lord Jesus Christ.

Bible Teaching

The two disciples on this road are among the first to come face-to-face with the risen Savior. Their response is one of growing faith.

◀ 24:13-27. The news of the resurrection stuns Jesus' disciples. As they scatter, two disciples are walking to a village just outside Jerusalem and discussing all that had happened. Jesus appears to them, but in such a way that they are prevented from recognizing Him (v. 16). As the disciples begin to talk with Him, they explain the nature of their grief to Jesus. Much of it was related to their hope that Jesus would be the physical restorer of the kingdom of Israel (v. 21). They lay all their doubts and fears before Jesus, including the puzzling reports about His resurrection. In response to their assessment, the Lord gives them a lesson in how to rightly interpret the Bible. One common mistake made in reading the Bible is to separate the Old and New Testaments. But here Jesus shows their connection. The Bible is one book. In the Old Testament, Moses and the Prophets predict the Messiah's mission and arrival, looking forward to His coming. By contrast, the New Testament looks back to Christ and describes and interprets His mission and arrival.

◀ 24:28-31. Next Jesus tests the disciples to see if their interest in Him is true. The disciples plead with Him to let them host Him for a meal. As Jesus eats with them, the scales fall from their eyes and they recognize Jesus. Yet His new body is different. Jesus, in His resurrected body, immediately vanishes from their sight.

◀ 24:32-35. The disciples not only recognize Him, but also His message. Instead of pondering over what it means, they now have certainty. They immediately return to Jerusalem, probably a 1.5 hour walk, and tell the eleven disciples what has happened. But their news is not surprising to those in Jerusalem. Jesus did not only appear to the two disciples, but also to Simon Peter, the very one who had denied knowing Him. As the accounts of His resurrection are multiplying, so is the faith of the disciples.

Family Discussion
Talk about the centrality of Christ in the Scripture's message.

Little Children: Talk to your little ones about how the Bible is one book. Show them how some of it speaks of Jesus before He has come and other parts about Jesus after He comes. Show how all of it talks about Jesus' work of dying for sinners.

Middle Children: Talk about how Jesus clarifies the disciples' thinking by teaching them the Scriptures. Talk about the Bible as the foundation for a proper understanding of belief and practice. How does the disciples' response to Jesus' words show the beginning of a growing faith among them?

Older Children: Look at Jesus' use of the Old Testament (Moses and the Prophets) to show His mission and office. Talk about the sacrificial system of the Old Testament which shows our need for a Savior, for example Leviticus 16:1-10. Talk about passages like Isaiah 53 that describe Christ coming as the Redeemer of His people. Talk about how the Old and New Testaments speak of the same plan of salvation.

Family Singing
A Mighty Fortress Is Our God (Trinity Hymnal #92); That Man Is Blessed (Psalter #1A)

Family Prayer
Thank God for Christ. Thank God for the Scriptures and how they lead us to Christ.

CHAPTER 62

Jesus' Earthly Ministry Completed
TODAY'S READING: LUKE 24:36-53.

Introduction

Luke ends his book reassuring Theophilus that God's redemption was fully accomplished in Christ. His work is done, and now He returns to the Father, where He is seated at His right hand. But where the Son's presence ends, a reminder of the promised Holy Spirit is given.

Bible Teaching

In today's verses there is the gradual revelation of the truth to the disciples, the opening of their minds, and Christ's Ascension.

◄ 24:36-43. Even as the disciples discuss His recent appearances, Jesus suddenly appears to the disciples. He shows Himself alive and takes steps to assure His disciples that He is not simply a spirit. The wounds remain in His body, which reveal He is Jesus of Nazareth who hung on the Cross on Golgotha. He invites them to touch Him, something that cannot be done to a spirit. But the greatest evidence of His physical resurrection is that He eats. Eating is unique to physical, material beings. You must be made of stuff to be able to contain other stuff. Spirits cannot do so.

◄ 24:44-49. As Jesus tells them how the Scriptures, Moses, the Psalms, and the Prophets, speak of Him, He gives them something that they had missed to this point: the ability to understand. The words to date had been heard but not understood, seen but not recognized. Now Jesus sets the essence of His ministry before them: Jesus suffered and died, was raised on the third day, and works repentance in all kinds of people and forgives them. The disciples had seen this ministry accomplished. They will carry on His work, but are instructed to wait for the Holy Spirit before they begin. Luke will tell more about the work of Christ by the Spirit in the disciples in his second book to Theophilus, the book of Acts.

◄ 24:50-53. With opened minds and changed hearts, the disciples witness the Ascension. Before He is taken from them, Jesus blesses the disciples, meaning He proclaims God's divine favor upon them. As He makes the declaration, He is taken up into heaven. Jesus' work is complete, and His presence is required no more. The Holy Spirit is about to begin His work among God's people. But as the disciples await His arrival, recorded in Acts 2, they return to Jerusalem according to Jesus' instructions (cf. Acts 1:4). Their waiting is no longer the same though. The confusion and sadness are gone and replaced with joy and worship. They have witnessed the accomplishment of God's plan of redemption in Jesus Christ and wait for it to be applied by the Holy Spirit.

Family Discussion

Luke's summary of the essence of Jesus' ministry is very important. Take time to review it.

Little Children: Talk about how the Bible teaches them what they should believe. Ask your little ones if they believe Jesus died and rose from the dead. Talk about forgiveness and repentance. Show how these things are certain.

Middle Children: Ask your children if they can give you the summary of Jesus' ministry recorded in verses 46-47. Show how this summary tells what they are to believe, *and* how they should act. Discuss their motivation for action through the idea of repentance of sin.

Older Children: Since Luke's stated purpose was to give Theophilus assurance (Luke 1:4), talk about the significance of the summary in verses 46-47. Discuss some ways in which Luke reassures his friend, and those who come after, of the gospel's message.

Family Singing

O Worship the King (Trinity Hymnal #2); Who With God Most High Finds Shelter (Psalter #91A)

Family Prayer

Thank God for sending His Son to suffer, die, and be raised. Thank Him for His forgiveness and for changing your heart.

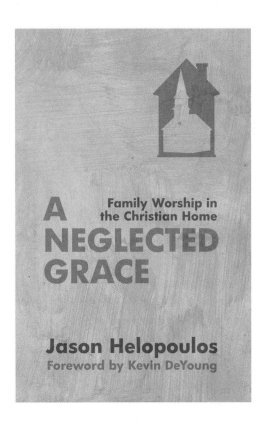

Family Worship in the Christian Home

A NEGLECTED GRACE

Jason Helopoulos
Foreword by Kevin DeYoung

A Neglected Grace

by Jason Helopoulos

Pastor Jason Helopoulos calls parents and church leaders to reclaim the practice of family worship. This indispensable means of grace directs our children to seek Christ daily, preparing them to go out into the world as fully functioning Christian adults, who love Christ and see all of life in relation to Him.

ISBN 978-1-78191-203-4

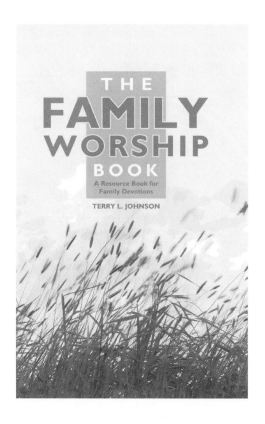

The Family Worship Book

by Terry L. Johnson

Do you struggle to provide enjoyable, meaningful and spiritual times of family devotions? Do you avoid the whole subject but have the nagging thought that you should be doing something?

Let Terry & Family Worship equip you for leading your family in worship with the help of some key questions: What is family worship? What have other people done? Why should I do it? How can I start? A valuable resource which you will not exhaust in years.

ISBN 978-1-85792-401-5

Let the Children Worship

by Jason Helopoulos

Jason Helopoulos encourages the church to embrace the important part children play in the life of the church and unfolds the enormous blessings to be found in having them present in the worship services of the congregation. He points out how the struggles are temporary – whereas the blessings can be eternal.

ISBN 978-1-78191-909-5

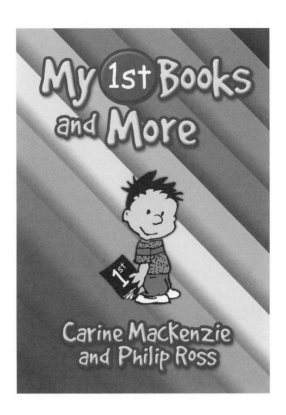

My First Books and More

by Carine Mackenzie and Philip S. Ross

Who is God? What does He do? Can I know Jesus? Why did He die? Children always have questions about God. They want to know what it means to be a Christian and who Jesus is.

This book takes the very popular children's series: My First and combines them into one colorful volume, with a new and exciting section on the Psalms. My First Books and More gives a year's worth and more of Bible readings, devotions and memory verses.

ISBN 978-1-78191-748-0